"What a timely read! It's so rare to find a book that is this theologically rich and carefully crafted yet rooted in the messy, churned-up earth of everyday life. A clarion call to justice, peace, and good old-fashioned laughter, Shalom Sistas will leave you changed. It's a book I can recommend to friends across the political and cultural spectrum—not because it is safe but because it is profoundly, prophetically true."
—RACHEL HELD EVANS, AUTHOR OF *SEARCHING FOR SUNDAY* AND *A YEAR OF BIBLICAL WOMANHOOD*

"You are going to love Osheta Moore. She is the best sort of friend for this journey of shalom: funny, warm, welcoming, challenging, wise, strong, and real. Osheta gives us the tools and practices to begin to live out our deepest longings for the kingdom of God in the midst of our messy, imperfect lives."
—SARAH BESSEY, AUTHOR OF *OUT OF SORTS: MAKING PEACE WITH AN EVOLVING FAITH*

"Over the years, I have continually learned from Osheta Moore's writing and witness, and Shalom Sistas is no different! Osheta has a gift for blazing a path toward liberation, hope, and purpose in any circumstance—in times of leisure or stress, abundance or scarcity, clarity or confusion. All people—not just women—will benefit from Osheta's careful and wise guidance through the complex intersection of faith, family, and community."
—CHRISTENA CLEVELAND, AUTHOR OF *DISUNITY IN CHRIST*

"Shalom Sistas made me want to stand up and cheer! Only Osheta Moore could land these powerful soul truths with such humor and grace. This hopeful manifesto is guaranteed to move you—to action, to peace, and ultimately toward the weird way of Jesus, where the gospel upsets our tired ideas and compels us to greater love."
—SHANNAN MARTIN, AUTHOR OF *FALLING FREE*

"All the jazz hands for this book! Shalom Sistas is the book we all need right now. Osheta Moore will make you laugh, challenge you, and offer you a practical path to peacemaking. You will want to be her friend and show up at her house for red beans and rice. I used to think peacemakers were supposed to be super nice and compliant, but no more. Osheta's shalom is strong and opinionated; there's nothing passive or saccharine about it. Shalom Sistas shows us the way."
—MELANIE DALE, AUTHOR OF *IT'S NOT FAIR* AND *WOMEN ARE SCARY*

"*Thank you, Osheta Moore, for capturing the joyful challenge of being a peacemaker in such a tangible way! By painting a beautiful, raw picture of living in the kingdom, Shalom Sistas will shake up your conceptions of what it means to follow Jesus.*"
—BRUXY CAVEY, AUTHOR OF *REUNION* AND TEACHING PASTOR AT THE MEETING HOUSE

"*God calls us beyond the surface kinds of friendships we've gotten used to and invites us into the richness of deeply meaningful relationships—even (especially?) with people we'd rather not get to know. Shalom Sistas extends the invitation once again, because clearly, God is not giving up on us.*"
—DEIDRA RIGGS, AUTHOR OF *ONE* AND *EVERY LITTLE THING*

"*I am so grateful for Osheta Moore's sassy voice, calling forth the Shalom Sistas of our generation. She invites us to practice ordinary acts of peace and to join her on this most crucial journey of peacemaking, rather than peacekeeping. And to think it all started with a dangerous prayer. She's my kind of woman, and I love her book.*"
—IDELETTE MCVICKER, FOUNDER OF *SHELOVES* MAGAZINE

"*In a world often wrought with unrest, Shalom Sistas offers a compelling way forward, calling the reader to consider what it means to live as peacemakers and not merely peacekeepers. Osheta Moore does this by giving us an intimate glimpse into her own story—weaving together personal narrative, humor, and just plain down-to-earth girl talk. A must-read for all who are determined to find and create life-giving spaces in the midst of chaos!*"
—GAIL SONG BANTUM, EXECUTIVE PASTOR OF QUEST CHURCH

"*As the divisions in our world get wider and deeper, the need for peacemakers—not mere peacekeepers—is stronger than ever. In Shalom Sistas, Osheta Moore offers honest, practical, and vulnerable wisdom and experience on how we can actively create shalom in our circles. Filled with real stories and tangible practices, this book will challenge, encourage, and strengthen readers to respond to God's call and bravely engage in the beautiful kingdom work of peacemaking.*"
—KATHY ESCOBAR, AUTHOR OF *FAITH SHIFT* AND COPASTOR OF THE REFUGE

"*Osheta Moore is the leader I want to follow. She loves God and is passionate about building God's kingdom on earth as it is in heaven. Her good heart and sharp mind are matched by her willingness to do the hard things as she seeks shalom right where she is planted. If you are committed to seeking shalom right where you are,* Shalom Sistas *can show you how.*"
—MARGOT STARBUCK, AUTHOR OF *SMALL THINGS WITH GREAT LOVE* AND COAUTHOR OF *OVERPLAYED*

"*Shalom is one of my favorite concepts in the Bible. It means complete reconciliation, the fullness of human flourishing, the state where humans express our humanness as it was meant to be. Sound heady? It is. Yet Osheta Moore writes about it in the same voice she uses when she calls up a girlfriend from the carpool line. I want to put my phone on speaker and chat with her all day. This is an important yet approachable read.*"
—JESSICA HONEGGER, FOUNDER OF NOONDAY COLLECTIONS

"Shalom Sistas *is a practical, engaging, theologically informed, poignant, and witty presentation of what peacemaking can look like in our time. Anyone who reads* Shalom Sistas—*no matter their level of theological understanding—will be challenged and encouraged to make peacemaking more than just an idea but rather an integral part of everyday life.*"
—DENNIS R. EDWARDS, SENIOR PASTOR OF SANCTUARY COVENANT CHURCH

"*Don't even think about using a highlighter as you read* Shalom Sistas. *You'll end up with entire pages colored in neon yellow! Instead, sit down with a cup of coffee, an open heart, and a box of tissues. Osheta Moore writes with conviction and humor about God's invitation to be a peacemaker.*"
—KATHY KHANG, COAUTHOR OF *MORE THAN SERVING TEA*

"*Strolling through the pages of Osheta Moore's* Shalom Sistas *is like taking a long walk with a dear friend. Relatable, brave, witty, and inspiring, this intimate work educates and empowers women to seek shalom in every aspect of their lives.*"
—JESSICA KELLEY, AUTHOR OF *LORD WILLING?*

"Osheta Moore is the Sista everyone wishes they had, and this book is packed with the Sista advice all of us need. Gloriously filled to the brim with Osheta's wit, wisdom, courage, and beautiful honesty, Shalom Sistas *challenges and propels me toward a joy-infused life of peacemaking for years to come."*
—JERUSALEM GREER, AUTHOR OF *AT HOME IN THIS LIFE*

"Osheta Moore reminds us all that peacemaking happens in the ordinary spaces of life. Readers will be brought to tears—sometimes due to uncontrollable laughter, and other times due to 'ugly cries'— but always with an empowered sense that peace starts here, now, with me! Read this book, if you dare, but beware: you might just become convinced that shalom seeking is for regular folks in regular places."
—KURT WILLEMS, PASTOR OF PANGEA CHURCH AND PODCASTER AT THEOLOGY CURATOR

"Osheta Moore breathes hope into the daily lives of women by exposing the hidden revolution at the heart of the ordinary. With a perfect blend of sass and grace, Osheta casts a vision for a world-rocking peace that takes shape one laundry load at a time."
—MEGHAN GOOD, TEACHING PASTOR AT TRINITY MENNONITE CHURCH

"Shalom Sistas *reorients our daily Christian practice toward God's dream of shalom. Osheta Moore is thoughtful and down-to-earth, and thankfully, the God she speaks about looks and sounds like Jesus. Her life-giving words are inspiring, and her transparent stories are striking and exquisitely written. In an age of despair and violence such as ours, this storied manifesto is a necessary encouragement for women (and men)."*
—DREW G. I. HART, AUTHOR OF *TROUBLE I'VE SEEN* AND ASSISTANT PROFESSOR OF THEOLOGY AT MESSIAH COLLEGE

"I can't remember a book I've waited for with more anticipation than Osheta Moore's Shalom Sistas. *Osheta's writing and teaching have revolutionized my life and my way of being in this broken world, and the heartbeat of her message is one that we desperately need in the church and in our culture. The pages of this book show that shalom is not some ethereal ideal, lovely in thought but impossible in practice; rather, shalom can be a real-life reality in the midst of every day. Osheta's approach to the active, engaged, and vital work of peacemaking has the potential to change our world."*
—MEGAN TIETZ, CREATOR AND HOST OF *SORTA AWESOME* PODCAST

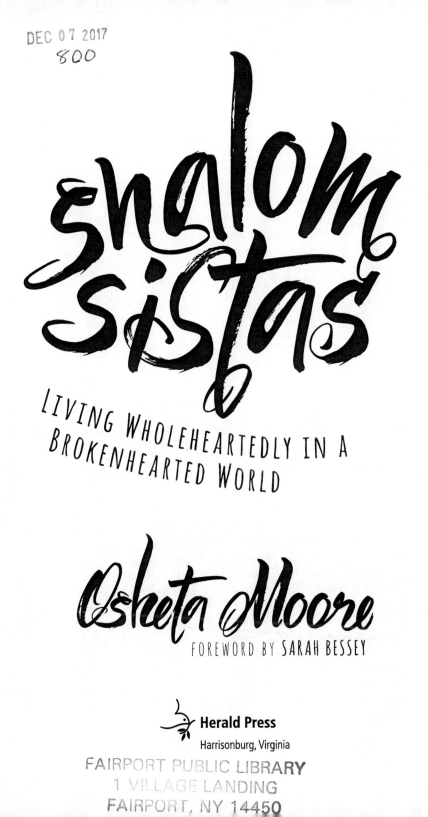

shalom sistas

LIVING WHOLEHEARTEDLY IN A BROKENHEARTED WORLD

Osheta Moore

FOREWORD BY SARAH BESSEY

Herald Press

Harrisonburg, Virginia

Library of Congress Cataloging-in-Publication Data

Names: Moore, Osheta, author.
Title: Shalom Sistas : living wholeheartedly in a brokenhearted world /
    Osheta Moore.
Description: Harrisonburg : Herald Press, 2017. | Includes bibliographical
    references.
Identifiers: LCCN 2017019272| ISBN 9781513801490 (pbk. : alk. paper) |
ISBN
    9781513801513 (hardcover : alk. paper)
Subjects: LCSH: Christian life. | Christian women—Religious life. |
    Reconciliation—Religious aspects—Christianity. | Peace—Religious
    aspects--Christianity. | City missions.
Classification: LCC BV4501.3 .M6655 2017 | DDC 261.8/73—dc23 LC
record available at https://lccn.loc.gov/2017019272

SHALOM SISTAS
© 2017 by Osheta Moore. Released by Herald Press Harrisonburg, Virginia
    22802. 800-245-7894. All rights reserved.
Library of Congress Control Number: 2017019272
International Standard Book Number: 978-1-5138-0149-0 (paperback);
    978-1-5138-0151-3 (hardcover); 978-1-5138-0150-6 (ebook)
Printed in United States of America
Cover and interior design by Reuben Graham
Cover photo by NataliaMills / iStock / Thinkstock

21 20 19 18 17   10 9 8 7 6 5 4 3 2 1

For my daughter, Trinity.

*May you find your place with Mommy
and all the Shalom Sistas
as we lead a revolution for peace.*

ven though he knew he would suffer, God had a plan—a magnificent dream. One day, he would get his children back. . . . God would love his children—with a Never Stopping, Never Giving Up, Unbreaking, Always and Forever Love. . . . Before they left the garden, God whispered a promise to Adam and Eve: "It will not always be so! I will come to rescue you! And when I do, I'm going to do battle against the snake. I'll get rid of sin and the dark and the sadness you let in here. I'm coming back for you!" And he would. One day, God himself would come.

—*The Jesus Storybook Bible*

Contents

FOREWORD

According to a Chinese proverb, "When sleeping women wake, mountains move." And in these days, I believe we're seeing this come to pass. Women are waking up.

All around the world, we are waking up to the real needs and experiences of the world thumping alongside our carpool lanes and hospital rounds, our budget meetings and class schedules, our boardrooms and our bedrooms. We are awakening to what charismatics like me call "the powers and principalities" of this world: racism, sexism, economic injustice, climate change, colonialism, consumerism, violence, nationalism masquerading as faith, and so on. We are awakening to our vocations, to our passions, to our joy and our anger, to our pain and our delight. We are awakening to what poet Mary Oliver calls our "one wild and precious life," and we can hear the voice of Jesus calling in the wilderness. We are awakening to the invitation of the Holy Spirit to participate with God in the redemption, resurrection, and restoration of all things.

But too often we wake up and immediately think: Yes . . . *someday*. *Someday* I'm really going to do something about this! *Someday* I'll change the world!

Oh, I know all about *someday*. And so we put too much of our awakening on hold because we think that these big things—shalom, peacemaking, resurrection—are the work of *someday* when we've got our life together.

Your *someday* is likely different from mine, but we all have a *someday*: someday when we're less busy (ha!), someday when we're married, someday when we have babies, someday when the kids are in school all day, someday when those babies are grown up and out of the house, someday when we retire, someday when we get our dream job, someday when we finally manage to go to seminary, someday when we can travel the world, someday when we have more money, someday when our responsibilities lessen, someday when we don't have to punch the clock, someday when we are preaching on stages, someday when we're ordained, someday when we're living in another country or culture, someday someday *someday*.

But someday never comes. We shush our longing for peace, our longing for wholeness, our longing for healing, for justice, for goodness, for love, in hope of someday. We end up feeling awake but stuck, awake but ineffective, awake but unengaged. Which is heartbreaking.

In *Shalom Sistas*, Osheta Moore gives us a tremendous gift: the bridge between our right-now life and those biggest hopes, dreams, and longings for this life. Osheta honors our awakening, and instead of saying "Yes, someday, you'll do something about that!" she gives us the tools, theology, practice, and community for moving mountains right *now*.

Osheta teaches us how to translate our big ideals into our daily realities. Small acts of faith and justice and shalom are still acts of faith and justice and shalom.

Oh, you are going to love Osheta. I first got to know her through her incredible blog *Shalom in the City*, but we became friends when she began to write for *A Deeper Story*, a magazine I helped to edit. Osheta is that rare leader who is staunchly alongside instead of ahead. She is the best sort of friend for this journey: funny, warm, welcoming, challenging, wise, strong, and real. She is deeply connected to her family and to her community and to the world and to Jesus. But she's her own person too: quirky and intentional, self-deprecating and soulful. I love everything she writes, because she writes just how she talks. There isn't any "Book Osheta" versus "Real-Life Osheta"; she's the same on the page as she is off the page.

Osheta's words here consistently gave me permission: permission to care instead of becoming numb, permission to challenge the status quo instead of going along with "the way things have always been," permission to honor my awakenings by being *fully* awake today, permission to bring my full, complicated, and whole self into the work of peacemaking in this world instead of fitting into some weird, stereotypical "good Christian lady" box. It turns out that, to be a Shalom Sista, we don't have to pretend to be someone we're not. We don't have to wait for someday, either.

Becoming a Shalom Sista myself has been life changing. Because of Osheta's leadership, I feel like someday is actually *right now*. There isn't a "someday" for peacemaking: we need only eyes to see, ears to hear, and hearts to understand.

Osheta gives us the tools and practices to begin to live out our deepest longings for the kingdom of God and to become part of the healing of the world in the midst of our messy, imperfect, real-right-now lives. I mean, honestly: the Shalom Sista Manifesto alone made me want to simultaneously lie down and cry and stand up and cheer. I wanted to run a lap, and I wanted to get to work.

There is no shame in this book. There is no measuring stick to show you where you're lacking, there is no to-do list or "You should really . . . " side-eye. There is only empowerment and embrace, hope and renewal here for you, Sister. I invite you to come on in. We're so happy you're here. This is our work: yours, mine, and Osheta's. We're Shalom Sistas: we are waking up, and now we have mountains to move.

—Sarah Bessey,
author of *Jesus Feminist* and *Out of Sorts: Making Peace with an Evolving Faith*

PART I

Shalom after the Storm

Not Your Typical Peacemaker

I see love rising like a hurricane.
    —Lisa Gungor

Kevin called today," my husband whispered in the dark. I couldn't see T. C.'s face, so I propped myself up on my pillow and moved closer to him, careful not to squish the toddler and unborn baby between us.

It was one week after we had evacuated from New Orleans, and all four of us were sharing a queen bed in my godparents' home in Texas. The evacuation had been mandatory. We wouldn't have left the city we loved had it not been for forecasters' promise that the storm was to be a Category 5 hurricane. We almost hadn't even listened to the mayor's speech, in which he predicted that if the hurricane hit the city, it would be devastating.

But I was eight months pregnant, and that had made all the difference. Hurricanes tend to down power lines leaving those poor souls who stay behind without air conditioning and refrigeration— this is a pregnant woman's nightmare. When we realized this, I told T. C. that for the sake of sanity and our marriage, it was best that we evacuate right quick and in a hurry.

We thought we were going to have a short visit with my god-parents in Texas, return to New Orleans and sweep up some debris, and then get back to our very busy, very meaningful lives. We were urban missionaries in Hollygrove, an underresourced neighborhood of New Orleans known for its gang violence. T. C. served as a literacy tutor in a local school and taught job skills to kids at a community center. As an ex–gang member, he was passionate about giving the guys a way to earn money that used their, um, sales experience for something positive. When I wasn't a pregnant, waddling, klutzy danger to myself and my unborn child, I put my years of training and college studies in ballet to work at the community center. I taught dance for young girls at the center, and since we all had to eat anyway, I occasionally hosted Sunday dinners at our apartment.

We were a young family seeking the peace of our city, with degrees in urban ministry to back it up. It was all very sexy, sensational, and incarnational urban core development.

Bless our hearts. We weren't expecting to lose everything in the costliest natural disaster in U.S. history. We weren't expecting all of it to come crashing down.

* * *

Now, for the first time since Hurricane Katrina had made landfall, T. C. wanted to talk. Like most married couples with little kids, we were having this life-changing conversation in bed late at night. T. C. didn't turn to look at me, which was a bad sign. It meant he couldn't process both the bad news and my reaction simultaneously, so he trained his gaze on the ceiling.

The light from the hall did solemn things to his face as he told me about his phone call with Kevin, our landlord and the director of the community center where we worked. Kids from our neighborhood had had to be rescued from their rooftops. The center would need extensive repair.

My brain transformed the sounds into words, but my heart could not comprehend their meaning. The ordeal was wearing on T. C. too, I could tell; a five o'clock shadow replaced his well-kept chinstrap beard. He swallowed and reached for my hand.

"Babes," I whispered, not wanting to ask the question. "What about our apartment?"

"Property owners were let back into the city to inspect the damage. The building took water up to the second floor, so our apartment is flooded." He paused. "Most of our things are useless now. They're either water damaged or smashed up."

I watched his lips move. Our building flooded? Most of our things destroyed?

"We need to figure out what we're going to do next," T. C. said. "We don't have a home in New Orleans to go to anymore."

Our two-year-old son stirred, and T. C. dropped a kiss on his forehead. "And until the center raises money for the rebuild, they can't pay staff anymore. So . . ." he trailed off.

"So you don't have a job anymore," I said completing his thought for him.

All of it was gone. Our life as urban peacemakers was ravaged by the storm.

He nodded and returned his gaze to the ceiling. "Tomorrow, Kevin wants me to email a list of things we lost in the storm. He's going to see if he can get us some help replacing them from donors."

Not knowing what to do with all my sadness and fear, I got up to start the list of things we lost. Even though I hadn't slept a full night since the evacuation, T. C. didn't stop me. He knew my Type A personality needed to wrangle chaos into bullet point lists and tidy little boxes.

I sat down at the computer in the dark and went to a website for evacuees, sponsored by an insurance company, and began to fill out the form. "Enter below the items you lost in the natural disaster," the website instructed in big blue letters.

Furniture: All of it. A two-bedroom apartment's worth. Everything. Beds, our new dining room table, which I had saved up for months to buy! My husband's man chair. Our son's big-boy bed. All of it.

Clothing: We evacuated a storm with only a day's notice! We only took three days' worth of clothes for a toddler, a grown man, and a very pregnant woman. Wouldn't you? I guess in a couple of months I'll need post-pregnancy clothes, because by the grace of God, I will have this baby.

Appliances: Well . . . everything. You think Hurricane Katrina was mindful that our landlord just bought that dishwasher? Nope.

For fifteen minutes, I filled out each field with a list of things we lost in the storm and just a tiny bit of snark. (Lord, bless and keep the poor agent who was on the other end of that web form.)

When I was finished, I submitted it and printed a copy for myself. Reading it over, I realized there was really no need for all that sass. Everything could, in fact, be replaced, except for a few gifts and art pieces we loved.

Though, the thing I was most saddened to lose was an artistic rendering of our family's life verse. The verse, Jeremiah 29:7, was on book pages that I made myself without the help of Pinterest, thankyouverymuch. It read: "Seek the peace and prosperity of the city to which I have carried you into exile. Pray to the Lord for it, because if it prospers, you too will prosper."

I had made the sign years earlier, after attending a lecture on God's heart for the city in preparation to enter urban ministry. I was struck by the speaker's love for community development and his explanation of a word that was new to me.

"Shalom," the speaker had said, "is what Jeremiah is invoking when he tells us to seek the peace of our cities. It is a picture of justice and wholeness for a broken city. In this verse, God is calling every one of us to be peacemakers for our city. Seek its shalom!"

As he introduced this biblical concept to us, I was relieved. Jesus' teaching on peacemakers had always rubbed me the wrong way, but the way this speaker taught us about shalom was refreshing— so much so that it began to shape both my ministry philosophy as an urban missionary and my picture of what it means to be a peacemaker.

In case you couldn't tell from my penchant to criticize dumb forms as I fill them out, I am not your typical peacemaker. *Peacemaker* has always been a problematic word for me. I don't want to be limited to peacemakers' eternal sweetness and quiet passivity. No, I want to be able to speak sarcasm fluently and to flip over a few tables in holy anger without the fear of Jesus giving me the divine side-eye for my misbehavior.

Also, I love Jesus, but I snark a little.

I'm usually not afraid of conflict, and ever since I saw Janet Jackson on MTV, I made it my life's mission to master the sassy head wobble in her "What Have You Done for Me Lately" music video. She is my patron saint of Don't Mess with Me, the fortifier of every woman who is not afraid of her sass. This was way before Beyoncé took to the stage, mind you. So please, before we go any further in this book: know that I'm not your typical peacemaker. And please, when we meet, ask me to teach you the head wobble. It is everything.

When I talk to my friends about peacemaking, two schools of thought emerge. Peacemaking, for many of us, is either/or. Either you're a peacemaker by *disposition*: a God-kissed person wearing a perpetual halo; you trade kindness for anger and gentle responses for harsh words. Or you are a peacemaker by *occupation*: you offer your body as a human shield in a war zone, mediate conflict between two people, or keep a world leader from typing in the nuclear codes. God help you if you don't fall into one of those categories. I guess you'll just have to aspire to a different beatitude from the Sermon on the Mount.

It's clear that I'm not your typical peacemaker by disposition, yet I want to be faithful to Jesus' teaching on peace, so I wholeheartedly threw myself into the occupation of peacemaking as described by the urban ministry pioneer. I was a peacemaker because I was "seeking the shalom" of a community in turmoil. I could harness all my anger and sass for the kingdom. Complete and total score.

If I'm honest, Sista—and I'm going to be honest, because I trust you're not going to start side-eyeing me at the outset of this book—I really loved the thrill of rightness I got as an urban peacemaker. I loved the impressed coos of approval I received when I told people of our work in New Orleans. Calling myself a peacemaker was not a declaration of my allegiance to Christ but an idol of my own making. Of course, it would come crashing down in the tempest of the storm.

Looking over that list of things we lost, my sadness over the ruined Jeremiah sign was deeper than I expected. That sign had become more than a daily inspiration. It had become a source of validation. Having that sign up, meant that when Jesus looked at me, he saw a peacemaker because I did all the right things.

So what qualified me as a peacemaker, now that the things I needed to convince me that I was one were submerged under ten feet of water? The one space where I had occupied the clear, heroic role of a peacemaker was gone. Who was I now?

* * *

Several years after the storm I stood at my kitchen sink in Cambridge, Massachusetts, angry with God. It was an evening during Mardi Gras, and a friend in New Orleans had sent me a picture of kids, all with purple, green, and gold face paint. "Wish you were here," the caption read. The kids with big smiling faces were some the kids we had loved and fed around our table just a few years before. The common room decorated with dozens of balloons was where I once taught dance. We used to be the ones who helped at the center's Mardi Gras party. That text was a frustrating reminder that my friend had gone back to seek the peace of the city we loved. I, on the other hand, had given up my peacemaking cred.

Our baby was due in less than a month, so we planned to just stay with my family in Texas. But shortly after we got the news that we lost everything, we got an exciting offer from a school in Boston with an urban ministry campus. Through an unlikely course of events and lots of tear-filled conversations, we decided to move to Boston. We could move to Boston and T. C. could attend Gordon-Conwell Theological Seminary, which both accepted his education grant from his work at the center and offered his ideal degree: a master of arts in urban missions. The seminary verified that it would accept him on short notice after the storm but only if he enrolled immediately. We were desperate for direction and a sense of purpose after the storm, so New England it was. Two weeks after the storm, we packed up our minivan for a massive road trip from Texas to Boston.

Once we got to Boston, we settled in quickly. As Hurricane Katrina evacuees, we were moved to the top of a two-year waiting list for public housing and placed in a comfortable townhome in Cambridge just ten minutes from Harvard University. Because of our evacuee status, we were offered a subsidy, so for the first six months we only paid a hundred dollars a month for a three-bedroom, one-bath townhome in a public housing development. It's amazing what doors nationwide news coverage of a hurricane can open for you.

With every year that passed, it became clear we were not moving back to New Orleans. On his way out to class that evening, T. C. had asked me how I felt about staying in Boston after graduation. I'll tell you more about this later in the book, but I experienced postpartum depression after my third pregnancy—a reality that forced T. C. to eat the elephant of seminary one bite at a time. Six years after the storm, he was still working on his degree. I told him that I loved Boston, I really did, but I felt that I was only a mom. I worried that I had no purpose other than to bundle up the kids, perfect an apple pie recipe, shovel our elderly neighbor's walk, and wash dishes. I wasn't an urban missionary or a peacemaker for my city anymore. I was simply me, and that sure wasn't enough.

I knew T. C. wanted to stay in Boston, and I did too. I just wanted to know what to do with all my love for the city and hopes for its wholeness when I was nestled in a little suburb in Cambridge.

My husband left and another hurricane with another manda-tory evacuation was coming, Sista. This time a hurricane of love, God's love was rising like a storm to force me to take a new way. You see, Hurricane Katrina forced me into a season of exile from the thing that defined me. Standing at the sink, I admitted to myself that I just wanted to go back to Egypt, where I was at least fed with my self-satisfaction and good works.

But God knew shalom was waiting in the wilderness.

* * *

The problem with starting out as a peacemaker in such a sensa-tional manner is that when you have to figure out how to dial back, nothing measures up. I was so desperate for the same min-istry I had in New Orleans that I reached out to new friends in Boston who were doing the very things we had done in New Orle-ans: incarnational living, entrepreneurship classes, and mentoring. I asked them for advice about how I could reinvent my urban peacemaking missionary life here, in this new place.

They suggested partnering with their nonprofit, which did sim-ilar work in Boston, and I said, "Of course! Just let me know what you need!" . . . and then found out that we were pregnant again. Two months after having our evacuation baby. Two pregnancies within the same calendar year. Which meant I wouldn't be part-nering with anything but Huggies and leggings for the next two years at least.

When mentors back in New Orleans invited us to give to groups committed to rebuilding the city, we sat down and looked at our budget. There was a reason we depended on subsidized housing and food stamps while my husband balanced work and seminary. Even with that help, we could barely make ends meet in a city that regularly makes the "highest cost of living" top ten list. Quite simply, we could not afford to give anything above our monthly tithes to our local church.

So that night at my kitchen sink I deeply missed my urban peacemaking life in New Orleans. I wondered how to translate my work as a peacemaker to our new city with our expanding brood. My husband was at class, and I was home with three kids—now ages nine, six, and five—praying angry prayers. I caught sight of my reflection in the kitchen window and saw traces of Cheetos dust on my forehead from my snack binge after a particularly stressful bedtime routine. I knew this was not a good look when one was taking on God with an existential rant. But hell hath no fury like a woman who receives a text that inspires a tremendous fear of missing out.

"I'm so over this, God," I muttered through gritted teeth while washing plastic dinner plates. I thought of my friends who had gone back to the city to help clean up and build houses for our neighbors and felt ashamed for not womaning-up and returning to the city with my baby strapped to my back and my toddler with a child-sized shovel in hand.

"I'm over feeling 'less than,'" I continued into the suds. "I'm over not knowing what to do with all this passion for peace and justice and no practical ways to live it out. Like. Over. It. Why would you give me a desire to work for peace and then take away all opportunities to do it?"

Later that night, T. C. came home and told me that he knew what he was giving up for Lent. The forty-day season directly after Ash Wednesday, Lent is a time of letting go of something good in order to lay hold of something that is better. Thanks to conversations with some Dietrich Bonhoeffer–loving seminary friends of his, T. C. had decided to give up Facebook for the next forty days. He wanted to see what would happen if he stepped away from the groups that defined him as a theologian so that he could grab hold of his true identity as a child of God.

Good for him, I thought.

Me? I told him I was mad at God and I wasn't a hundred percent sure why.

"Do you think that if I fast from something this Lent, Jesus and I will be cool again?" I asked. "Maybe then I won't be so mad that we lost everything in the storm. I really hate this anger. Jesus can be annoying, but I still miss him."

"No, I don't think it works that way, babers," T. C. said. "And when you don't get the answer you expect, I think you'll be more hurt because you'll believe God didn't come through for you. I don't want that for you." He put his hands on my shoulders and met my eyes. "What you need to figure out is what is keeping you from connecting with him from an authentic place and then give that up for Lent. Lent is an invitation for God to take the place of that one thing that keeps us from him."

He kissed my cheek, pointed out the traces of Cheetos on my forehead, and went to check on the kids.

Sitting down on our couch, I stared at the verse that started it all: Jeremiah 29:7. (You better believe I replaced that Bible-verse art as soon as I had time and energy to. In its current iteration, it was written on a supertrendy chalkboard because Martha Stewart told me to.) "Seek the peace and prosperity of the city to which I have carried you into exile. Pray to the Lord for it, because if it prospers, you too will prosper."

Seek. Pray. Prosper. What wonderfully active words, yes. But the potential for failure was staggering. I was most assuredly not at peace.

Looking at the sign, I realized that I couldn't connect with God from an authentic place because I felt that he had sold me a bill of goods with this whole peace thing. I was angry at God because I wanted him to bless my striving for peacemaking perfection in our new city, and he wasn't.

For so long, I believed peace could be attained through what I did and what I accomplished. But in truth, Hurricane Katrina forced me to question my motives and calling to be a peacemaker.

I thought about what my husband said. For Lent, he was giving up something that he believed defined him in order to lay hold of his true identity.

Suddenly, the idea came to me. I defined myself as a seeker of shalom, a peacemaker for my city, and so much of my identity was wrapped up in that. What if my Lenten observation was to make peace with the peace teachings of Jesus? Would that recalibrate my identity and calling so that I experienced more purpose in my efforts towards peacemaking and less insecurity? I hoped so. With this newfound purpose, I devised a plan.

For Lent, I would give up my preconceived notions of peace in order to find something better. For its forty days, I would study every mention of peace in the Bible. I really wanted to find out what Jesus meant when he said, "Blessed are the peacemakers, for they will be called children of God" (Matthew 5:9). I would read what theologians had to say about it and listen to sermons by ministers I trusted. Hopefully by Easter Sunday, I would have a better understanding of how to be a peacemaker.

With my plan in place, I brushed the Cheeto dust off my forehead, looked at the remade sign of Jeremiah 29:7 and prayed a dangerous prayer.

"Jesus!" I said. "I have no idea what this Scripture means for me as a peacemaker anymore. Seeking the peace of my city must mean more than I thought it did. Obviously, I've got this all wrong. So come on . . . show me the things that make for peace."

✷ ✷ ✷

Maybe you're like me and you think peacemaking is not for you. You love Jesus and snark too. You're in a season of caring for little ones, and peacemaking to you means shutting down a kid's conniption in the Target aisle with café popcorn and a Capri Sun. Possibly you aren't planning to move to Syria anytime soon to help with the refugee crisis. Possibly you're wondering, can I be a peacemaker right here in my safe little life?

This book is a resounding yes. *Shalom Sistas* is about how we can claim our place among the blessed peacemakers. It reveals a third way of peacemaking that doesn't require us to be peaceful by disposition or by occupation. It describes a kind of living that doesn't ask us to be someone or something we are not. Together, we'll explore the way of shalom and the practices of the whole-hearted. *Shalom Sistas* is about the anthem of the kingdom of God and our pledge of allegiance to the Prince of Peace centered on one word that kept coming up over and over again during the forty days after I prayed that prayer.

During that Lenten season, which I called my Forty Days of Peace, this one word continually set me free from comparison to the Mother Teresas and Nelson Mandelas of the world. It uncovered a liberating concept that still to this day encourages me to fully live into my unique ability to be a peacemaker right where I am, every single moment, in ordinary yet meaningful ways.

Shalom. The Hebrew word often translated as "peace" in the Bible, shalom is God's dream for the world as it should be: whole, vibrant, flourishing, unified, and yes, at peace. Shalom is God's dream for his love to bring wholeness and goodness to the world and everything within it, including you and me. In our effort to make this word accessible to our everyday lives, we often miss out on this richer view.

Maybe you own a piece of art with the word *peace* on it that you hang on the wall at Christmas. Maybe you exclaimed to your own kids just this morning, "Can I have some peace and quiet, please!" Like many people, you've read about conflict in the Middle East and have wished an end to war. Maybe you have tried not to whisper the corny catchphrase, but it escapes your lips anyway: "Lord, let there be peace on earth." We want our dead to rest in peace, we ask our therapists to help us achieve inner peace, and many of us end our emails with one word: peace.

And so when you hear *shalom*, you immediately think it means peace . . . which isn't too far off. Except it's that thinking that had me angry with God and mourning the loss of our ministry for several years after the storm. What I've learned since then is that peace is not a thing to achieve. It's a way of being.

Shalom is a "persistent vision of joy, well-being, harmony, and prosperity," writes theologian Walter Brueggemann, a vision with "many dimensions and subtle nuances: love, loyalty, grace, salvation, justice, blessing, righteousness." Shalom is "the freight of a dream of God that resists all our tendencies to division, hostility, fear, drivenness, and misery."

Shalom is more than avoiding conflict or feeling inner calm—although it can include both.

"We understand peace to be the *absence* of conflict," writes Rob Bell. "We talk about peace in the home or in the world or giving peace a chance. But the Hebraic understanding of shalom is far more than just the absence of conflict or strife. Shalom is the presence of the goodness of God. It's the presence of wholeness, completeness."

Shalom is the breadth, depth, climate, and smell of the kingdom of God. It's a counter-story, with nothing missing and nothing lost for everyone who reads it. We become peacemakers when we, through the guidance of the Holy Spirit, catch glimpses of shalom, and pull our friends to stand in our line of vision so that they too can see the beauty of the kingdom.

Shalom is what happens when the love of God meets our most tender places. Therefore, we can all be peacemakers, because we can all seek and access the love of God to heal our broken places.

This is what I've learned, Sista, through my forty days of wandering through Scriptures and sermons and books about shalom. Unless love rises up like a hurricane and disrupts our comfort, bringing to the surface all the ways we've been brokenhearted, we can never live wholeheartedly. We can never truly seek peace, shalom, and wholeness for those around us. *Shalom Sistas* is our mandatory evacuation from views of peacemaking that constantly leave us feeling "less than."

But, you may ask, isn't peacemaking about impressive, large-scale conflict resolution and fixing the world's problems? Sure, I guess. But let me ask you this: If you are not at peace first—if your definition of peacemaking is dependent on others' needs being met first—is it really peacemaking, or is it hustling for your worthiness? Let's consider the dreams God dreams for us: that we be women who love wholeheartedly because we were first wholly loved by a good God.

* * *

Now, I know you're probably leaning back with this book in your lap, thinking, "Mmm . . . girl, I don't know. We got real serious there, didn't we? You're telling me peacemaking starts with the heart. Are you planning to share your deepest, darkest heartaches in this book? Do I need some tissues?" Yeah, maybe.

We're going to talk about all the ways we feel so brokenhearted in this world. Let's get honest about how body shame and skin privilege has left us grasping for acceptance. Let's address the obvious frustrations of how to love a God we cannot see, and what to do when we feel that he has abandoned us.

Once our broken hearts have been made whole, we can't help but seek wholeness for others. We've felt the warmth of the sun in the kingdom of God, and we can't stand the idea of a whole world shivering in the darkness. When that happens, you better get ready. When that happens, we become people who run toward conflict, not away from it.

So we'll talk about some of the more traditional acts of peacemaking too. We'll talk about loving our enemies and resisting division and why I really wanted to sleep with a baseball bat under my pillow when the Boston bombers fled into my neighborhood.

Don't get me wrong: while shalom brings peace, it is also active and alive. In my forty days of peace, I became convinced that peacemakers are not pliable, passive, or permissive.

Peace is fierce—it has to be, because violence and discord won't go down without a fight. Those who wield peace in the face of the world's violence do it fiercely. And yes, some of us are even prone to flip some tables over when we see injustice. Can you blame us? We've seen how, in the kingdom of God, people matter and how the marginalized have a special place in Jesus' heart. Plus, Jesus flipped some tables, so why can't we? A servant cannot be less than her master, right? Right.

Shalom is aggressive and audacious, and it's accessible to you and to me. So I started calling myself a Shalom Sista, in addition to a peacemaker. A Shalom Sista is a woman who loves people, follows the Prince of Peace, and never gives up her sass. Shalom Sistas are not well-behaved, tame women, because peace is not a thing that can be tamed. Calling myself a Shalom Sista meant I focused on fully living into God's dream of wholeness for me in a brokenhearted world.

We'll also go over the Shalom Sista Manifesto: twelve guideposts for living wholeheartedly in this brokenhearted world. You'll get to see some peacemaking fails and successes as I attempted to live out each manifesto point. If shalom is the culture of the kingdom of God, then you and I are its ambassadors. And if we are ambassadors, the Shalom Sista Manifesto will serve as our rules for engagement.

This book is not an exhaustive tome on shalom. What I learned during those Forty Days of Peace is that one cannot exhaust the boundaries of the kingdom of God. One cannot write a little book on shalom and call it a day. I know so many people who write dissertations and plan whole seminary courses on shalom. *Shalom Sistas* is a collection of stories about how I ran toward the goodness of God with my broken heart and how he made it whole again.

And really, if you strip away all the trappings of peacemaking as a disposition or an occupation, you'll see that is what the best peacemakers do: make their corner of the world a little more whole and welcoming than it was before they came on the scene.

I wanna be that bringer of peace: the shalom of God. If you're reading this book, I think you do too. If you believe the world can be a unified and better place, you are a Shalom Sista.

If your heart aches and you want more for yourself and your world, then you, my dear, are perfectly poised to receive the shalom of God. He's eager to show you his love, his devotion, his completeness right where you are, right this very moment.

And in case you're wondering if you can get away with calling yourself a Shalom *Sister* instead of a Shalom *Sista*, I'll say this: it's up to you. My husband says that the older I get, the thicker my Southern accent becomes. I'm just this side of sounding like M'Lynn Eatenton from *Steel Magnolias*. He's caught me extending the *i* when I say rice, and my *y'alls* are way more pronounced than ever. Whatever. I'm owning it. So when I say *sister*, it inevitably comes out *sista*. Know this, sweet Sista: if *sister* is more comfortable for you, just go with it. This is a shame-free sisterhood!

Join me, Shalom Sista, in exploring the ways you and I can see shalom in our contexts in meaningful and accessible ways. We're going to have a lot of fun, and I might share a recipe or two. Because shalom requires me to bring my whole self, I'm going to have a sense of humor about peacemaking and a willingness to share my worst failures: like how I nearly went angry-badger-mama crazy when a coach called my son the n-word. Or that time I threw a half-full bottle of formula at my husband's head because he wouldn't get up to do a 3:00 a.m. feeding. Or even the several months I spent using a portmanteau of Voldemort and the name of a woman I really, really didn't like simply because she had embarrassed me at work.

Being a Shalom Sista means being liberated from always getting this peacemaking thing right. But I want us to be confident ambassadors of the love of God, so at the end of the book, you'll see a section called "Shalom Steps." These are practical things you can do right now that will help you embrace the shalom of God right where you are. In this way, you can begin to see change in one of four areas: within your relationship with God, within yourself, within your relationships with the people in your life, and finally, within the world.

My prayer for you as you read *Shalom Sistas* is that you'll know that you are uniquely gifted to create wholeness and goodness right where you are. You don't have to have the job or the disposition of a peacemaker. You just need to have the desire to see God's radical peace invade every ordinary corner of your life. Let us be women who seek peace because it's part of our spiritual inheritance as daughters of God, not because it may give us the thrill of self-righteousness. Let us be ambassadors of the kingdom, anthropologists of its transformative ways. Let us be champions for justice, wise warriors, and eager reconcilers. Let us be women who love because we were first loved.

Let us be Shalom Sistas.

-2-

Forty Days of Peace

The kingdom of God is an alternative arrangement of human society around Jesus which leads to human flourishing.
—Brian Zahnd

It was a Wednesday night when I made up my mind to do Forty Days of Peace. By Sunday afternoon, I had stacks of Bibles and books on peace, shalom, and Jesus scattered everywhere around my kitchen. The counters and the chairs were full, and pieces of my children's art served as bookmarks: a hand-drawn family portrait holding the space in Isaiah, a handprint Thanksgiving turkey pointing me to Jewish commentary on shalom, a Joan Miro–inspired page of line art featuring bends and curves marking the Sermon on the Mount.

Just for Lent, I took the cookbook I was working through down from its stand and replaced it with Walter Brueggemann's *Living toward a Vision: Biblical Reflections on Shalom.* Every once in a while as I passed by, I could get a nugget of insight on what, exactly, shalom is and how I could integrate it into my life. The kitchen table became my office, and when the family went to bed, I studied. During the day, while the kids were in school, I'd walk laps around Fresh Pond, a park in Cambridge, and listen to every sermon I could on Jesus' teachings on the kingdom of God.

The very foundation on which I had stood for so many years—my understanding of peace and of Jesus' role in my life—was shifting. Old ideas were fusing with new concepts. I felt the change coming the same way you sense when a childhood friendship crosses the threshold into adulthood. You perceive the change coming as you go through the college graduations, the marriages, the babies. But then suddenly you're sitting across from each other, all heck breaking loose around you as your kiddos play, and you realize: We're older. We're talking about grown-up things now. Our friendship has matured.

My friendship with Jesus was coming to that threshold. You see, I never really stopped to ask myself why I called him my Prince of Peace. I mean, other than its awesome alliterative properties, "Prince of Peace" meant nothing to my modern, democratic, post-Enlightenment mind.

To be clear, I am a woman who loves peace and desires to be a peacemaker. Jesus is my favorite teacher, thinker, leader, lover, fighter, Savior—all of it. So if he who restored my sense of worth and identity says something offbeat like "Love your enemies" and "Put away your sword," and if he says that I must know the "things which make for peace" (Luke 19:42 NASB), I listen. When I call him my Prince of Peace, it's not just a flowery title. I really believe that Jesus brings peace into every circumstance in my life.

But what if the title "Prince of Peace" pointed not just to Jesus' desire for me to cast my burdens upon him because he cares? What if "Prince of Peace" had something to do with Jesus' mission on earth too?

* * *

"Show me the things that make for peace," I had prayed that Thursday night. The prayer comes from Luke 19, where we find that peace and the kingdom of God are inextricably linked. Jesus was not only on a mission to bring comfort to a suffering world; Jesus was revealing that the culture of his kingdom stood in a stark contrast to the kingdom of the world, which often facilitates that very suffering.

The Luke 19 account is one of the few times we see Jesus weeping. This time, he wept as he entered Jerusalem on what has come to be known as Palm Sunday.

> And they brought [the colt] to Jesus, and throwing their cloaks on the colt, they set Jesus on it. And as he rode along, they spread their cloaks on the road. As he was drawing near—already on the way down the Mount of Olives—the whole multitude of his disciples began to rejoice and praise God with a loud voice for all the mighty works that they had seen, saying, "Blessed is the King who comes in the name of the Lord! Peace in heaven and glory in the highest!" And some of the Pharisees in the crowd said to him, "Teacher, rebuke your disciples." He answered, "I tell you, if these were silent, the very stones would cry out." And when he drew near and saw the city, he wept over it, saying, "Would that you, even you, had known on this day the things that make for peace!" (Luke 19:35-42 ESV)

Palm Sunday is the occasion on the Christian calendar when we commemorate Jesus' triumphal entry in Jerusalem. The concept of a triumph requires some explanation, because it's foreign to modern believers.

A triumph was a ceremonial and celebratory procession through the streets of a city. When the Romans wanted to celebrate their latest conquest, they celebrated with a triumph. In fact, in 70 CE the Roman general Titus destroyed the very city into which Jesus entered that first Palm Sunday. Titus's triumph, with the spoils from the Jerusalem temple, is depicted on a monument that remains in Rome to this day.

That first Palm Sunday, Jesus wasn't the only person leading a procession into Jerusalem. There was another one coming from the opposite side of the city. Pontius Pilate entered Jerusalem from his home in Caesarea. His procession was in the Roman style—complete with a terrifying display of Rome's military might. Pilate was perched atop a majestic stallion, and he had all the trappings of Roman wealth and prestige. His procession was a proclamation of his and Rome's superiority. And it came with an undeniable message directed to the pilgrims who had gathered in the city from near and far for the Passover festivities: "Keep the peace, or we will control you by force!"

Meanwhile, on the other side of the city, many gathered to celebrate and welcome Jesus. To them, this was his triumphal entry because they thought he was coming into Jerusalem to establish the kingdom of God. Soon all would be set right, they believed. Shalom would come again! And they were right, in a way. But Jesus' triumph was of an altogether different kind than they expected. He was establishing the kingdom of God, a way of being that was vastly different from any earthly kingdom. His victory would not be won by military might. His status would not be secured by wealth or prestige.

Pontius Pilate entered on a stallion, representing the kingdom and power of Rome, while Jesus entered on a gentle, humble donkey, representing the kingdom of God. This contrasting imagery arrested me and brought me back to a refrain from Jesus I read over and over again: "The kingdom of God has come near."

For three years, Jesus had been teaching, "The time has come . . . the kingdom of God has come near. Repent and believe the good news!" (Mark 1:15). Throughout his ministry, he reinforced this declaration by doing things that would identify him as the Messiah: a royal figure whom the Israelites believed would come and set up his kingdom here on earth.

Jesus riding into Jerusalem as king that day was particularly important for the Jews, because Israel was under Roman occupation. The Roman way of being and the Roman culture were dominant. Rome called all the shots. In fact, Romans were so taken by the success of their empire that this season of prosperity, born of war and domination, had a name: Pax Romana, or "the peace of Rome." When someone invoked the term Pax Romana, the listener would immediately see a montage of Rome's conquests. They'd see images of centurions forcing civilians to carry their equipment,

Roman coins with the image of Caesar hailing himself as the son of God, and yes, even crosses along major thoroughfares with anyone who rebelled against Rome nailed to the wood, raised up, and gasping for their last breaths. Because of Pax Romana, Caesar was sometimes called "King of Kings," "Lord of Lords," and—yes, y'all, you beat me to it—"Prince of Peace."

Then Jesus came on the scene to usher in the inbreaking beauty of the kingdom of God. By doing so, Jesus exposed Rome for what it was: empire's desperate grasp for power and its complete lack of decency or humanity.

As the Messiah and Son of God, Jesus began setting up the kingdom of God on earth in ways that directly countered Rome, which confused the Jewish leaders hoping for a Messiah formidable enough to take on Rome. They had lots of misunderstandings about what the Messiah would do to liberate Israel. They believed the Messiah would come to destroy the oppressive regime in the same way that a normal regime rose to power: through force, finances, and defilement of its enemies' core values.

But Jesus wasn't having any of that. No, in his ministry he went about setting up his kingdom differently, because his kingdom of God *is* different than earthly kingdoms. For three years, Jesus taught us a counterstory and modeled a counterculture for his followers. The Jewish leaders should have been paying closer attention, because the prophet Isaiah had told them how God planned to establish his kingdom and restore shalom to the earth. It had to be vastly different from the way the Roman Empire was going about it.

In the last days

the mountain of the Lord's temple will be established

as the highest of the mountains;

it will be exalted above the hills,

and all nations will stream to it.

Many peoples will come and say,

"Come, let us go up to the mountain of the Lord,

to the temple of the God of Jacob.

He will teach us his ways,

so that we may walk in his paths."

The law will go out from Zion,

the word of the Lord from Jerusalem.

He will judge between the nations

and will settle disputes for many peoples.

They will beat their swords into plowshares

and their spears into pruning hooks.

Nation will not take up sword against nation,

nor will they train for war anymore.

Come, descendants of Jacob,

let us walk in the light of the Lord.

(Isaiah 2:1-5)

As the world superpower of the day, Rome embodied everything that was wrong with the world. And Jesus had to wreck shop in order to set up the shalom of the kingdom of God on earth.

Where Rome esteemed hierarchy and status, Jesus revealed the image of God in all people and made friends with the marginalized.

Where Rome practiced law and order, Jesus preached enemy love and nonviolence.

Where Rome intimidated with torture and execution, Jesus liberated by healing the sick and, ultimately, dying on the cross. This modeled the core ethic of his kingdom: sacrificial love.

Jesus was crucified not because he was a nerdy theologian who annoyed the campus bully. He was crucified because he was a radical who was mobilizing people to question, engage, and hold earthly empires accountable for their violence.

In Jesus' invitation to see the shalom of God, we begin to see the truth. Empires are never truly helpful in securing our peace, and we must repent of our empire ways. Jesus posed a very real threat to Pax Romana. But that's okay, because the peace of the kingdom had, in fact, come near.

So Jesus—Son of God, our true Prince of Peace—rode on a borrowed colt into the city where he would die at the hands of a violent empire. In so doing, he put on display the contrast between the peace found in the kingdom of God and the peace we manufacture in this world.

This misunderstanding—that peace is a thing that we obtain by control or manipulation—is why I never felt that I could be a peacemaker. Turns out that praying to learn the things that make for peace included, for me, learning a new understanding of the kingdom of God.

Jesus' triumphal entry as Messiah was just the beginning of my understanding of shalom. Good Friday and Jesus' coronation as king of his altogether different kingdom was coming.

It was time to look closely at the cross.

* * *

I used to believe that peace was a byproduct of following Jesus and escaping the fires of hell. I was raised in a Pentecostal church that gave me a healthy respect for the wrath of God. That wrath was so clearly poured out on Jesus on the cross, right?

His death, I was told, bought me my salvation and appeased an angry God. His death as an innocent contrasted against my guilt so vividly that I should fall to my knees in gratitude. His death was excruciating and horrific, so I should love him all the more. His death saved me from hell so that I could spend forever with him. Because of the cross, peace would come from heaven, which I now had access to because I was saved. So much centered on the death of Jesus as punishment for my sins and for evil in the world that I never thought to pay attention to his love, his acceptance, his overcoming of evil.

It's hard to see the glory when you're consistently presented with the gruesome.

But being a follower of Jesus requires us to look at the whole of his life: his birth, his childhood (as much as we know of it), his ministry, how he spoke to people, where he ate, where he rested, and where he performed miracles. Being a follower of Jesus means embracing a blessing found in the Mishnah, a Jewish commentary: "May you be covered in the dust of your Rabbi."

So while the blood of Jesus covers my sins, I want the dust from his sandals to cover my life.

We lose sight of our true calling as followers of Jesus if we pay attention to only one moment—his death—and divorce it from the whole of his example. It's like listening to the last five minutes of a professor's lecture and then assuming you know the whole scope of her class.

No, Jesus was way more strategic and thoughtful than that. He, being fully God and fully human, could do what none of us could: show us how to live the culture of the kingdom of God here on the earth.

This is why Jesus said, "I am the way and the truth and the life. No one comes to the Father except through me" (John 14:6). Jesus' greatest goal was to show us the way of the Father, to give us a glimpse of the kingdom of God, and then empower us to live right here on earth. Jesus' mission was to usher in shalom.

When Jesus said these words, he was telling us that the kingdom of God has come through him and his example.

> The Spirit of the Lord is upon Me,
> Because He anointed Me to preach the gospel to the poor.
> He has sent Me to proclaim release to the captives,
> And recovery of sight to the blind,
> To set free those who are oppressed,
> To proclaim the favorable year of the Lord.
> (Luke 4:18-19 NASB)

Shalom is the Lord's favor, and it is among us now! We do not have to live lives bound up in misery, oppression, ignorance, and fear. We know that peace has come because Jesus brought the culture of the kingdom of God with him to show it to us.

All of this puts the cross in a new light for me. The cross is the culmination of Jesus' ambassadorship of the kingdom of God. The cross saves me not just because Jesus covered my sins with his innocence; the cross saves me because it invites me to be loved and known by the God who would rather die for me than live all eternity without me. This is the highest, greatest value of the kingdom of God: sacrificial love. This is how God brings about our shalom. In light of this, shalom is more than surface-level peace; it is a deep, running river flowing with selfless love. That love then secures our peace.

I had to step back and, as an anthropologist of sorts, wander around the kingdom of God and pay attention. I had to carefully notice Jesus' words and actions, and to see them as indicators of the core values of the kingdom—the things that make for peace in the kingdom of God. I landed on one driving thought: shalom is the culture of the kingdom of God.

As I began paying deeper attention to Jesus' whole life, it became clear that he was deeply concerned with how we live. In his invitation to the disciples—twelve men from different backgrounds, with competing ideologies, and each passionate about healing the brokenness of the world—he said, "Follow me." Not "Believe what I believe." Not "Espouse the right doctrines." Jesus said, "Follow me." We are to follow his example because he is the way of healing and wholeness for the world. He is the only agent of true peace, shalom, for people then and for us today.

This means that while I was forming a new orthodoxy—correct beliefs about peace centered on the Hebraic concept of shalom—I also had to focus on shaping my ortho*praxy*—correct practices of shalom.

In an interview about the kingdom of God, Dave Tomlinson, author of *How to Be a Bad Christian*, said, "[When] Jesus said, I am the way, the truth and the life, he didn't say, 'this is a doctrine about the way, the truth, and the life or a doctrine about Jesus Christ. No, he said that it was him; it was the way and the truth that he embodied and lived and demonstrated and led and liberated people."

Jesus embodied the shalom of the kingdom of God, and we are called to do so right here and right now. If shalom is the culture of the kingdom of God, then being a Shalom Sista means translating key components of the culture of kingdom of God into actions here on earth.

* * *

I know a few things about translating a culture that is not my own into my everyday life. I've lived in three distinctly different cities, and each one has influenced me.

Even now, years after we left, components of New Orleans culture come out in my everyday life. I season everything with Tony Chachere's Creole Seasoning—although I stop short at ice cream, because that's just gross. When something exciting happens, I turn on trombone-infused jazz and dance around, recreating a second line, of sorts, in my living room. If my husband is taking longer than he promised to bring a gallon of milk home from the store, I'll text: "Where y'at?" And I know that man reads it with a Cajun accent, even though neither one of us truly has one.

And every Monday, I still make New Orleans red beans and rice. I first made red beans and rice the day after we moved into the Hollygrove neighborhood of New Orleans. The night before T. C. started a new job at the local elementary school as a literacy tutor, I was on the phone with a woman from church named Cathy. "Well, while your husband is off working for the day, you can get your beans and laundry done," Cathy said.

"What?" I asked.

She laughed. "Oh, that's right: you're not from here!" She cleared her throat and began to teach me the ways of New Orleans cooking, starting with red beans and rice.

Red beans and rice is a New Orleans staple (you'll find the recipe on page 232). Go to any hole-in-the-wall restaurant in Louisiana and you'll find the cook's version of red beans and rice. It's simple: soaked beans, onion, garlic, bay leaf, and seasonings. If you have it on hand or company's coming, you can add sausage, or ham hock, or bacon. Red beans are flexible like that. Their simplicity makes them the perfect meal. You assemble it all in a pot, bring it to a boil, turn the heat down low, and go about your business. Several hours later, dinner is ready.

Because it's so no-fuss but has a big impact, red beans and rice is the perfect meal for the days when you have lots of housework to do. In fact, the tradition of making red beans on Mondays started back when homemakers washed their family's clothes by hand. They would have piles of laundry to wash but lots of bellies to fill as well. So Mondays were washday, and red beans were on the menu.

I loved this tradition so much. After Cathy wove that recipe with story and a connection to the vibrant culture of New Orleans, I immediately rushed to the Piggly Wiggly and bought the ingredients.

Years later, the ingredients for this dish were on the very first grocery store list I made when we were Hurricane Katrina evacuees in Cambridge, Massachusetts. Ever since that call with Cathy, except for illness, vacations, or invitations to dine out with friends, I've made red beans and rice on Mondays. Even now, here in Los Angeles, I make it. To be honest, I didn't want to come out the gate as the new pastor's wife with a Southern accent who makes red beans and rice—I mean, how cliché! But old habits do die hard, and after we moved here I found myself adding the ingredients to our shopping list every week. And since it's his favorite meal, our son T. J. chooses it for his birthday dinner every year, whooping with excitement when he walks into the kitchen and smells the beans cooking on the stove.

As the beans simmer and the house fills with the spicy, warm, rich scent of beans and sausage coming together to make the most perfect thick and creamy soup, it often feels like New Orleans, even though I'm in Los Angeles.

Once a week, I give my family a taste of New Orleans. Once a week, I'm reminded of the culture that I love. It's comforting to know that a little piece of the Big Easy is with me wherever I go.

Just as I carry the culture of New Orleans with me, a Shalom Sista carries the culture of the kingdom of God with her wherever she goes. It comforts, guides, and empowers us as we seek to be peacemakers for ourselves and the world. We do this because we first saw Jesus, our Prince of Peace, embody the culture of the kingdom of God. Sarah Bessey writes of our calling as shalom seekers so beautifully in *Out of Sorts: Making Peace with an Evolving Faith*.

> In the Kingdom of God, we join with God in co-creation, in the work of the new earth. We love and we follow Jesus. We shape our lives into His life, to live here on earth as He would live among us. We weren't called to follow political parties or ideology, nationalism, consumerism, or power. Instead, we were called to apprentice ourselves to Jesus' way of life. We were called to be part of establishing the Kingdom of God here and now in our walking-around lives. Partnering with God to see the Kingdom come.

So how, exactly, could I live as a kingdom woman in my everyday life?

-3-

THE SHALOM SISTA MANIFESTO

Lord, make me an instrument of your peace:
where there is hatred, let me sow love;
where there is injury, pardon;
where there is doubt, faith;
where there is despair, hope;
where there is darkness, light;
where there is sadness, joy.
—**Prayer of Saint Francis**

It is a truth universally acknowledged that a millennial woman in possession of a life verse or a particularly moving quote from, say, Rumi or Oprah, will be in want of a way to memorialize it.

Top considerations include (1) a blog, (2) a piece of artwork made from reclaimed wood or restored metal, and (3) a tattoo.

Near the end of my Forty Days of Peace experiment, I had two out of three.

"Babes!" I called to T. C., who was working on a seminary paper in the man chair replacement I had bought as soon as we got to Boston. "I'm gonna start a new blog."

"That's what? Blog number three?" he called back. "First was the mommy blog, and then the urban ministry blog. What is this one going to be about?"

I rolled my eyes and sucked my teeth at his sarcasm. "A shalom blog! A kingdom blog. One blog to rule them all!" I announced. Because yes, gentle reader, as a millennial, I must tell all the Internet that big things were happening in my neck of the woods.

T. C. was quiet for a beat, then responded from the other room, "That might be a hard sell, babers." (He calls me babers. I call him babes. I have no idea when this started.) "Shalom and the kingdom of God are pretty big concepts, plus you still really do love the city. How are you going to tie those together?"

"Hmm," I started, as I wrote blog title ideas in my journal. "Well . . . how about Shalom City? Like Sin City, but a play on words."

T. C. got up from the comfort of his chair to stand at the doorway between our kitchen and living room. He gave me the flattest, most unimpressed deadpan look ever known to husbands. "Shalom City?" he repeated. It sounded even worse coming from him.

"Okay, it's pretty bad. I know! Give me a minute." He checked his phone for the time, crossed his arms, leaned against the doorframe, and waited. Deadpan still in effect. That man is impossibly literal at times.

I scribbled "Shalom" and a combination of ideas for the blog with the same enthusiasm I had when I first met T. C. and dreamed up different configurations of my first name with our lasts.

Feeling his interest slip away, I flipped to a page of notes from a book that referenced Saint Augustine of Hippo's *The City of God*. My eyes fell on the quotation that had initially drawn me to the book:

> It is this Good which we are commanded to love with our whole heart, with our whole mind, and with all our strength. It is toward this Good that we should be led by those who love us, and toward this Good we should lead those whom we love. In this way, we fulfill the commandments on which depend the whole Law and the Prophets: "Thou shalt love the Lord Thy God with thy whole heart, and thy whole soul, and with thy whole mind"; and "Thou shalt love thy neighbor as thyself."

I was also intrigued by the distinction Augustine makes between the "city of God" and the "city of man." This was a pastoral response to early Christians, who were afraid for the future of Christianity and their potential persecution after the fall of Rome to the Visigoths around 410 CE. Augustine was encouraging these early believers not to fear if earthly empires were to fall, because the city of God would triumph.

As a former urban missionary, I liked this language of city. As a Western thinker, I couldn't quite get my head around the concept of kingdom. When I hear the word *kingdom*, I think of *Game of Thrones* or a prince on a white steed declaring his undying love to a maiden—not a humble king riding in on a donkey, a king who displayed his love through serving the poor and dying on the cross. Both words—*kingdom* and *city*—are used by theologians to communicate how God intends to bring wholeness to where we feel broken and how God reorients our whole lives and society around his shalom. God's inbreaking goodness is as vast as a kingdom and as alive as a city.

The idea of a city also played to my personality. Even though I was raised in a Texas suburb, I have been and will always be a city girl at heart. I know cities. I love cities. I agree with novelist Neil Gaiman, who writes, "Cities are not people. But, like people, cities have their own personalities. A city has identity and personality." Augustine similarly describes God's reign on earth as a city: one vibrant with his love, grace, and guidance. This vision made Jesus' teachings on the kingdom of God way more accessible to me.

With my husband leaning against the door, the clock counting down, and my mind whirring, I had one thought: If the city of God had a name that could describe its personality, what would it be?

Shalom.

Shalom expresses the complexity of the goodness of God with the practical application modeled by Jesus. That ache you feel, the sense that the world is not right? That's the shalom in the city of God calling us back home. Jeremiah 29:7 came full circle for me: "Also, seek the peace and prosperity of the city to which

I have carried you into exile. Pray to the Lord for it, because if it prospers, you too will prosper."

Not everyone is called to a physical city here on earth, but everyone can find wholeness in the city of God. Not everyone knows what it's like to physically live an exiled life—driven away from the land you and your ancestors love. But because sin entered the garden of Eden, we are all exiles from the city of God. In this world, there's a universal desire for rest. In every sigh, every tear, every disgusted exclamation and shake of the head over a world gone wrong, we are embodying the heartbreak of our exile from the city of God. We all want to make our way back home. What, then, does it look like to embody the shalom of the city we long for?

"Shalom in the City!" I announced to the waiting man.

He pursed his lips and stood up a bit straighter. He liked it, I could tell. But knowing my husband, he was also going to make me defend this decision. "Why?"

I told him about Augustine's city of God, and loving urban life, and embodying shalom and yearning for the garden of Eden. "We live out the kingdom of God on earth because Jesus told us to!" Between you and me, I added that last part in for good measure. Everyone knows Sunday school survival rule number one: add Jesus to your answer and you'll always get a cookie.

So T. C. bought the domain name Shalominthecity.com and quietly began building me a website.

And me? On Good Friday of my Forty Days of Peace, I recommitted myself to our humble King and got a tattoo of a dove on my right wrist.

Three for three.

＊　＊　＊

The *Shalom in the City* blog went live, and over the course of the next five years, I wrote about my broken heart and how it was being made whole. And it resonated. I discovered more women like me: mothers and single women, teachers and nurses, managers and at-home parents, all with big hearts for God, deep longings for peace, and totally average resources. What if these Sistas couldn't start an international shoe company for social justice or house all the homeless folks in the city? Was our only option to ignore Jesus' words about peace and give up any hope of joining in God's family business of peacemaking because, well, it's just an impossible task to live out?

Hundreds of women started writing to me. They said they never knew they could be peacemakers for themselves, and certainly not for the world. They told me they used to think that peacemakers were some special breed of Christian, but that they were beginning to think maybe they too had a role in God's shalom. They raised their hands and said, "I'm hurting too; thank you for putting my pain into words."

I spoke on the phone with Sistas from Ontario to North Carolina who had read something I wrote about God gardening with me when we lost our church plant, and how I needed to know I was beloved. They wanted to know: Is God truly that good, and can I really trust him? Short answers: Yes, and oh my goodness, yes! I shared about our work in the city, but I also wrote a letter to my sisters in the suburbs, asking forgiveness for the ways they've felt alienated by urban do-gooders who suggest that anyone who doesn't live in the city isn't truly faithful. I told them that geography is not a reliable indicator of fidelity. I could almost feel the pressure gauge of "I'm not enough" release, both for them and for me.

Years after I started the blog, I sat in a Starbucks in Cambridge with an acquaintance who wanted to say goodbye. We were moving to Los Angeles. T. C. had been offered a position as an associate pastor in what could only be described as our dream church community. Just weeks before, he had left to get settled into his job while I stayed home to pack up our apartment, get in a few more snow days, and give the kids a chance to say goodbye to their friends. I wrote on my blog about my anxieties about moving and how I missed my husband. I used the imagery of Jesus as our Good Shepherd and me as the sheep following behind him. I talked about the zigzag pattern of shalom—how sometimes it makes sense to me and sometimes it feels foolish, but it always inspires me to live wholeheartedly.

My friend, a pastor and professor with a master of divinity degree from Fuller Seminary, had lived near Los Angeles for a while, so she wanted to meet for coffee to send me off to the part of the country she loved with a prayer and an encouragement. She also wanted to debrief about the blog post I had written.

She pointed to a few lines in the post: "Being a Christian feels less like a to-do list of righteousness and more of a to-be posture of relationship. I want to be open to his feeding and present for his gathering. I want to be accepting of his gentle leading and willing to be carried."

"You figured it out, didn't you?" she said with a twinkle in her eyes, eyes beautifully lined with age and good humor.

Good thing I wasn't taking a sip of my latte at that moment or I would have spit it out all over this lovely woman. "I haven't figured anything out!" I exclaimed.

"No, listen," she said. "It's all about relationships. Shalom is about wholeness in every possible relationship we could have— with God, with ourselves, with the people in our lives, and with the world. When you write, you write about wholeness in relationships in these multiple directions. You point us to the kingdom of God and invite us to live in our relationships here on earth as if we're already in the kingdom. It's important, and it's what you figured out. I know it's so cliché, but being a Christian is about relationships instead of religion. Clichés become clichés because there's truth in them."

That acquaintance had no idea that Starbucks meeting would provide the framework of the Shalom Sista Manifesto: a twelve-point statement of how we live out the culture of the kingdom here on earth in four distinct areas. Shalom with God. Shalom with ourselves. Shalom in our relationships. Shalom in our world.

No finite list or manifesto can capture the infinite expression of the shalom of God. We are imperfect peacemakers trying to find our way, and our identities cannot be bound up in what we do or accomplish, as I learned when I thought I lost all my peacemaking cred during Hurricane Katrina. No. The Shalom Sista Manifesto is not a checklist for do-gooders; it is not a list of shoulds. My spiritual director once said to me, "There is no 'should,' Osheta. There only is right now. What do you need from God, right now?"

At the end the day, the manifesto nudges us toward practicing peace in those relationships right now. It challenges us to usher in the goodness, hope, and love of the city of God in small, practical, everyday ways. So many times, Jesus likened the kingdom of God to average things: mustard seeds, yeast, light, coins. There's a brilliance to his teaching that's important for us as we go through the Shalom Sista Manifesto. The potential to embody the kingdom of God is right here, right now, in our everyday life. It's not "out there," in the extravagant acts of peacemaking, but in the small things: the smile at a stranger, the honest journal entry, the forgiveness offered an errant child, the care package you take to a new mom.

It's our promise to be everyday peacemakers.

God marked the path for me, and wise theologians left signs along the way to keep me on track. But without the light of the Spirit guiding me, showing me the next right step, I would have stumbled and stubbed my toes and eventually given up on the journey altogether. I decided the best I could do as an imperfect peacemaker was to stand up and point out shalom in order to help my Sistas find their way. The manifesto is also a list of the ways that the city of earth has broken my heart and the ways that the city of God has healed it.

*　*　*

In *A Hidden Wholeness*, author Parker Palmer encourages us to look closely at our brokenheartedness and let it lead us to whole-hearted living. "Wholeness does not mean perfection," Palmer writes; "it means embracing brokenness as an integral part of life.

Knowing this gives me hope that human wholeness—mine, yours, ours—need not be a utopian dream, if we can use devastation as a seedbed for new life."

In our culture, we've been conditioned to run away from brokenheartedness. But in the kingdom of God, brokenness is beautiful, and wholeness comes when we lean into our breaking. When the woman with the alabaster jar wept, broken and vulnerable before Jesus, he called that act beautiful. In fact, it is the only time in the Bible that Jesus describes an act as beautiful. And take Jesus himself, who was coronated king on the cross and rose on the third day. He lived out another ethic of the kingdom of God: that we are broken by the same things that break God's heart. Then and only then we are made whole.

A Shalom Sista recognizes that brokenheartedness and wholehearted living are not opposites. No, we hold these things in tension. We're beautiful and we're broken. So as I crafted the manifesto points, I wanted to see brokenheartedness not as a thing to run from, but as a thing to learn from.

There's a curious line in the bridge of a song we sing at church that I never understood until I began studying shalom. The line asks God to break our hearts for the things that break his. The Shalom Sista manifesto helps us live out that prayer. We allow our hearts to break for the things that break God's so that we can be co-laborers for flourishing. In doing so, we live out our humanness at its fullest— heartbreak, pain, and all.

Weeks after that Starbucks date, I sat by a pool in Los Angeles while my kids swam, and I thought about the manifesto. I pulled out my journal and a new bright orange gel pen (because you can't help but smile when you see something written in bright orange).

I wrote:

"Our hearts break when we _____.

But in the kingdom of God, we _____.

So we _____."

Fifty statements came in that first draft. But fifty is a daunting number, and it would have made this book about five hundred pages long. So I stepped back and narrowed the list down to twelve. Twelve areas of heartbreak caused by the world's way of relating, and twelve resulting promises of wholeness, flourishing, goodness, and peace found in God's way of relating.

These twelve fall into four distinct relationships, what Lisa Sharon Harper calls concentric circles of relationships. "God's intent for the world is that all aspects of creation would live in forcefully good relationships with one another," Harper writes in her fantastic book on shalom, *The Very Good Gospel*. Forcefully good relationships: amen to that.

So here's the manifesto that forms the core of this book.

The first area in which I want to seek shalom is in my relationship with God.

1. Our hearts break when we believe God is displeased or angry with us. When our picture of God is anything but loving, good, and just, we're in danger of never truly finding wholeness in him. But in the kingdom of God, we look to Jesus for our clearest picture of God. So we are invited to love and be loved.

2. Our hearts break when we believe that we are not wanted and that we have no place in the world. But in the kingdom of God, we remain in God's love. So we are beloved.

3. Our hearts break when we feel that we are not enough so we believe in scarcity. But in the kingdom of God, there is flourishing, and goodness, and abundance. Jesus said, "I have come that they may have life, and have it to the full" (John 10:10). So we are enough.

The second area of seeking shalom is in my relationship with myself.

4. Our hearts break when we feel that our bodies and skin are unwanted, unlovely, or liabilities in this world. But in the kingdom of God, we know that God breathed his very image into humanity, which means every single person is an image-bearer of a beautiful God. So we will see the beauty.

5. Our hearts break when we tie our value to our production and run ourselves ragged in order to accomplish and gain more. But in the kingdom of God, rest and work have equal value; the

economy of God is measured by love and trust, not dollar signs and billable hours. So we will rest.

6. Our hearts break when we see injustices and feel overwhelmed by sadness all around. But in the kingdom of God, the melody of heaven persistently breaks into a dark world. So we will choose subversive joy.

The third area of relationships in which I want to see shalom is with others: the people in my life with whom I interact every day.

7. Our hearts break when a person we trust betrays us or when a group of people make choices that negatively affect us. They quickly become our enemies, and we tell stories in which our enemies are always the villains deserving of judgment. But in the kingdom of God, we love our enemies and pray for those who persecute us. Love gives nuance to their behavior and shifts us, as the victims, from the center of the narrative. So we will tell better stories.

8. Our hearts break when we give in to pride. When we're so aware of our gifts, so confident in the ways we can help, so eager to show off how amazing we truly are, we forget that we do not have to grapple for worth. But in the kingdom of God, the first are last and the last are made first—like Jesus, who "being in very nature God, did not consider equality with God something to be used to his own advantage; rather, he made himself nothing by taking the very nature of a servant" (Philippians 2:6-7). So we will serve before we speak.

9. Our hearts break when we give in to our fears that keep people at a distance. We embrace our prejudices and forget that every single person has immeasurable worth to God. But in the kingdom of God, Jesus is himself a bridge and has torn down the dividing wall of hostility between us and God. So we will build bridges, not walls.

The fourth and final area in which I want to see shalom flourish is in my relationship with broken systems in the world.

10. Our hearts break when we systematize love and put quotas on wholeness. But in the kingdom of God, God's goodness is

persistent and God's mercy follows us all our days. So we will choose ordinary acts of peace.

11. Our hearts break when we see injustice but are silent out of fear of disturbing the peace. But in the kingdom of God, Jesus has been coronated king on the cross, saying, "The Son of Man did not come to be served, but to serve, and to give his life as a ransom for many" (Mark 10:45). Jesus stands in solidarity with us when we are at our most broken, are most in need, are most vulnerable to the oppression of the world. So we will show up, say something, and be still.

12. Our hearts break when we see violence of any type—violent speech, violent actions, violent retaliation and self-preservation. But in the kingdom of God, we beat our swords into plowshares and refuse to use violence of any kind to achieve peace. We will rely on the creativity of the Holy Spirit. So we will be peacemakers, not peacekeepers.

✴ ✴ ✴

Lord knows twelve paragraphs could not easily fit on a reclaimed wood sign. So I wrote out twelve core beliefs and action steps that have shaped my practice as a Shalom Sista.

1: We are invited.
2: We are beloved.
3: We are enough.

4: We will see the beauty.
5: We will rest.
6: We will choose subversive joy.

7: We will tell better stories.
8: We will serve before we speak.
9: We will build bridges, not walls.

10: We will choose ordinary acts of peace.
11: We will show up, say something, and be still.
12: We will be peacemakers, not peacekeepers.

Can I tell you a secret? I'm not firing on all twelve cylinders of the Shalom Sista Manifesto every day. Neither should you. There are days I do well with telling better stories about others, but struggle to rest. Some days I'm all about my belovedness, but I still look in the mirror and think, "If only I could be a few pounds lighter, I'd really be beautiful."

In my practice of shalom, I identify with what Shonda Rhimes confessed in a graduation address at Dartmouth. People ask her how she does it all, she said in her speech. "The answer is this: I don't. Whenever you see me somewhere succeeding in one area of my life, that almost certainly means I am failing in another area of my life."

The same is true for me as a shalom practitioner. In fact, it's for this very reason that I started using the language of *practice* when it comes to peacemaking. Before you explore all the ways you can be an everyday peacemaker, it is essential you understand that some manifesto points will speak to you at some points in your life and not at others. Go with it. Girl, listen: If you naturally succeed in choosing joy, then guess what that means right now. Your babies, your friends, your community have one person in their midst who brightens their days, who reflects the joy of heaven here on earth. Don't tell me that's not a gift! Sure, you wanna learn to tell better stories; awesome, you'll get there. The Holy Spirit is in this for the long haul, so practice telling better stories until it becomes as second nature to you as your subversive joy.

"Shalom is something we seek every day," my friend Sarah said offhandedly one time. "It's a practice of peace, really, because we rarely get it right the first time. But Jesus helps us along, doesn't he?"

I aspire to be like Sarah. I like the idea that every day when I wake up, I can pray, "God, how can I practice shalom?" Living into the shalom of God is a learning process, and this book covers my favorite and most memorable lessons.

My hope is that the Shalom Sista Manifesto helps you identify the things that make for peace so that you can live wholeheartedly in a brokenhearted world. So let's get started.

Part II

Shalom with God

-4-

DANCE, BABY:
WE ARE INVITED

I feel so badly for people who come to this party of Christianity and refuse to dance. Why do we show up to the party and refuse to dance?
　—Glennon Doyle Melton

ould I borrow your God tonight?" The text message surprised me on my way to bed. It was from Brandy, a blog reader and longtime online friend. Whenever I notice readers commenting on my blog or in the Shalom Sista Facebook page, I try to take our online friendship offline. It only seems appropriate that I give them a chance to tell me their stories, since they've been so generous to listen to mine. I've had fascinating conversations on motherhood, race, football, the proper way to make black beans, graphic T-shirts, fair trade jewelry, and everything in between.

Brandy is one of those Sistas. As I wrote the Shalom Sistas Manifesto for the blog, I asked for her thoughts. She loved the idea, but she had one question: "Can I really be a peacemaker even though I'm not sure how I feel about God?"

I didn't anticipate her question, even though it's such a good one. I just assumed anyone who is interested in peace would, on some level, also be interested in God. (Thanks to my culturally Christian upbringing, I tend to assume that everyone believes what I do.)

That night, I sat cross-legged on my bed and crafted no fewer than four different responses to Brandy. Finally I settled on one that felt humble and honest.

"You don't have to borrow him, sweetie. He's already yours."

✳ ✳ ✳

If our understanding of shalom hinges on the goodness of God, what happens when we, like Brandy, don't believe God is good?

I came to faith in a charismatic church. So I know there's a temptation to shout down that uncertainty with "God is good . . . all the time. All the time . . . God is good!" But what happens if we think God is not good? What happens when we suffer and when we feel abandoned? In whom do we find peace when our lives are utterly chaotic?

Let's look closely at that uncertainty for a moment. In his book *The Sin of Certainty*, Peter Enns makes a case for examining our mistrust of God in order to grow in our faith. He writes, "When we reach that point where things simply make no sense, when our thinking about God and life no longer line up, when any sense of certainty is gone, and when we can find no reason to trust God but we still do, well, that is what trust looks like at its brightest—when all else is dark."

What is your mental picture of God, Sista? I don't mean to get all philosophical on you, but I really wanna know. Who we imagine God to be matters. The mental images we create about God can determine if we fall in love with him, grow to fear him, or become ambivalent about him. Our picture of God determines if we truly believe God is good and want his goodness in our lives. If we do not believe God is good, then entering into his shalom—God's dream for the world—will feel like a waste of time or, in some cases, dangerous. Why would we make ourselves vulnerable or uncomfortable for a God we're not even sure we can trust?

I believe God has invited us to partner with him to seek the shalom of the world. We are invited to become peacemakers. But before we accept the invitation, we need to examine our relationship with God and, perhaps even more importantly, our feelings about him. Do we feel scared of God? Anxious about him? Angry at him? Abandoned by him?

Trust me, Sista, I know the power of mental pictures very well. When T. C. and I first started dating, we lived far away from each other. He was in a pastoral internship in Champagne, Illinois, and I was finishing my third year of college in Denton, Texas. We had met on a short-term urban mission trip to New Orleans during Mardi Gras. After one week of serving alongside each other, we were officially twitterpated.

At the end of the week, before we went back to our respective homes, we swapped email addresses. We cultivated our romance over daily email exchanges. This was before everyone had their own laptop, so in between classes, I would go to the campus computer lab to see if he had emailed me when he got into the office that morning. For weeks, we played a *Jeopardy*-esque game to parse out each other's theology and love for the 1999 film: *The Matrix*. The winner received a rose made in ASCII art. ASCII art makes pictures out of the characters on the ASCII chart: commas, dashes, dollar signs, and certain letters or numbers. Yep, we're pretty much two nerds who fell in love. (Somebody get Rainbow Rowell on the phone—I have the plot for her next book!)

We eventually progressed to phone calls. Again, this was the olden days, so we didn't have Skype. If we wanted to "see" each other on our phone calls, we would play a game called Mental Picture. Now before you take your mind to a naughty place, Sista, just know that we as a couple had "kissed dating goodbye." We were way too holy to waste our precious courting phone calls on base sexual references. Bless my idealistic little heart. Honestly, though, our mental picture games stayed solidly PG.

We'd ask questions like "What's right outside your window?" "What's on your desk?" "Your TV?" "Your couch?" This game served two purposes: it made us feel close to each other, and it helped to paint a picture of the person we were falling in love with. With every detail T. C. gave me, he was inviting me to know more about him. The stack of sketchbooks on the corner of his table told me he was an artist. The wrinkles in his work shirt told me he had spent most of the day sitting in meetings. The television muted, with *Saturday Night Live* playing in the background, told me he valued laughter and quick thinking. These little glimpses into his life helped form a picture that reinforced my affection.

My mental pictures of T. C.—of good, kind, smart, and funny— would help to determine my acceptance of his proposal three years later.

We don't have the luxury of nightly phone calls with God. We can't hear God describe what's going on in his yard or what's sitting on his coffee table to help us shape our picture of him.

But we do have Jesus. Jesus is the perfect revelation of the character of God.

Hebrews 1 says:

God, after He spoke long ago to the fathers in the prophets in many portions and in many ways, in these last days has spoken to us in His Son, whom He appointed heir of all things, through whom also He made the world. And He is the radiance of His glory and the exact representation of His nature, and upholds all things by the word of His power. When He had made purification of sins, He sat down at the right hand of the Majesty on high, having become as much better than the angels, as He has inherited a more excellent name than they. (Hebrews 1:1-4 NASB)

Some of us find it hard to see Jesus when we think of God. When faced with the enormous task of explaining to each other a God we cannot see, we often rely on clichés that can do more harm than good. Here are my top four well-meaning but unhelpful church clichés:

Let go and let God. Does that mean God is like me in the kitchen when my daughter is trying to make chocolate chip cookies and she makes a total mess? Does God hover anxiously and then angrily send me to the other room so he can take over?

God doesn't give you more than you can handle. Wait. Hold up. Are you telling me God is a spiritual weightlifter, all buff and glistening, who stands over us and yells, "Give me one more rep!" Um . . . weightlifting is hard, and I like pie.

When God closes a door, he opens a window. So God is a celestial contractor who's obsessed with drafts? Cool, cool.

God helps those who helps themselves. If I'm understanding this clearly, then God is a scorekeeper who doesn't really care about people's needs. His super-divine help is appropriately doled out on the basis of notches and effort.

Look. I get the impulse to wrap the infinite that is God into our finite language. I do. I'm married to a pastor, and I've helped him craft a catchy one-liner or two. Pithy phrases for sermon prep are my jam! The problem comes when we base our picture of God on sayings like these instead of on the Word made flesh: Jesus.

When we rely on these clichés more than on the example of Jesus, we are like Philip the disciple, who said to Jesus, "Show us the Father and that will be enough for us" (John 14:8). Philip understood the fathers, the prophets, and the popular sayings of his day, but not this enigmatic teacher who spoke of the kingdom of God and who said that the way to the Father was through him. So he asked Jesus to just make it plain.

Jesus turned to them and said, "Have I been so long with you, and yet you have not come to know Me, Philip? He who has seen Me has seen the Father; how can you say, 'Show us the Father'? Do you not believe that I am in the Father, and the Father is in Me? The words that I say to you I do not speak on My own initiative, but the Father abiding in Me does His works. Believe Me that I am in the Father and the Father is in Me" (John 14:9-11 NASB).

Theologian N. T. Wright puts it like this in an interview: "If you want to know who God is, look at Jesus. If you want to know what it means to be human, look at Jesus. If you want to know what love is, look at Jesus. If you want to know what grief is, look at Jesus. And go on looking until you're not just a spectator, but you're actually part of the drama which has him as the central character."

Before we jump into the other manifesto points about living wholeheartedly, we have to know and trust the one who makes our wholeness possible—Jesus. Jesus, who said he has come so that we might have life to the full, is the exact embodiment of God the Father.

Let's take a quick look at the life of Jesus to give us a glimpse of the goodness of God. Jesus loved his enemies, challenged injustices, healed the sick, fed the hungry, taught the eager (women included), resisted patriarchy, rested his body, cared for the earth, celebrated, wept, and served. In a remarkable act of selfless love, he died on the cross, and in an even more remarkable act championing us against sin and death, he rose from the grave.

There's something so compelling about Jesus, but we're still a little hesitant about the Father, aren't we? This breaks my heart, because Jesus and the Father are not separate from one another. If Jesus is altogether good and lovely toward us, then so is the Father.

Brandy and I had been having a conversation about the Jesus-looking picture of God for weeks. I didn't know if I was getting anywhere with her—you rarely can tell in a texting conversation. But her request that night—to "borrow" my God—helped me realize that while most of us want to be on this path of peace and we're even open to including God in it, we have two hang-ups about him.

One: We rely on clichés about God as sovereign over our suffering or too holy to know us. God then feels either unreachable or terrifying. In this picture, God is a tyrant.

Two: Sometimes, when we try to look to Jesus as a picture of God, his life and example seem overwhelming to average people like us. With all the healing and feeding, loving and challenging, dying and resurrecting, it's just so unattainable.

How do you overcome the fear of God as tyrant or God as unattainable?

I'll tell you how: Magic. Comfort. Love. Joy.

Let me tell you a story about an invitation to dance under twinkling lights.

✳ ✳ ✳

A few years after we moved to Boston, T. C. and I were bitten by
the church-planting bug. We found ourselves longing for a new
kind of Christian community: urban, intentionally multiethnic,
intentionally multi-socioeconomic, and rooted in historic, litur-
gical practices. After years of being nurtured as leaders in some
wonderful congregations, we felt God calling us to form and lead
a new community. The Evangelical Covenant Church was the
denomination with which we felt full alignment in terms of values
and mission.

One of the cool things about planting with the Covenant is
that you get to meet with church planters in your region once
a month for encouragement. The network of support from sea-
soned planters as well as planters at our stage was one of the
main reasons we planted with the Covenant. In that group were
two Covenant pastors, Andrew and Corrie Mook, who invited
my husband to preach at Sanctuary Church, their congregation
in Providence, Rhode Island, one Sunday. We were both humbled
and thrilled.

The Mooks are some of our favorite people on earth. Corrie
is all life, love, and effervescence. Andrew is warmth, thoughtful-
ness, and passion. They've played Red Light, Green Light with
my high-energy kiddos on the cobblestoned streets of Providence.
When I had to be at a conference and flying out of Boston was too
expensive, I stayed at the Mooks' house and Andrew drove me
to the Providence airport at four in the morning. Their heart and
vision for Providence was so much like ours for Boston that whenever I was around them, I was a little bit in awe of God's provision.
By just living out their call to church planting, they confirmed that
the wild hopes and fantastic dreams for the city that God had
whispered in our ears were possible.

Visiting Sanctuary encouraged me for the future of our church
plant in the same way hanging out with a mom of grown child
gives me courage to persevere through the hard mothering of

tweens and teens. Yes, you can do this. No, you will not go to jail for smacking the sass right out of your thirteen-year-old's mouth, but it's probably not a good idea. Yes, they will still come back for laundry and pot roast. Yes, it's the most amazing thing ever!

"Yes, you can plant a church," the Mooks' example said to us. "Yes, the Holy Spirit will help you share the gospel effectively. Yes, this is the most amazing thing ever!" They gave us hope for urban church plants.

For several days before our visit to Sanctuary, I had been studying Hebrews 1, and I was becoming a hot mess. I was considering how my faith needed to shift if I were to adopt a Jesus-looking picture of God and move away from the tyrant God picture I had unintentionally accepted. I was ready for this shift the same way you're "ready" for a bikini wax: you know you need it to rock your suit with confidence, but still . . . yikes!

Hebrews 1 was asking me to focus on Jesus, and I wasn't sure I was ready for all that came with it. As a Shalom Sista, it's easy for me to say, "It's all about Jesus," but what does that mean, exactly? It's easy to be intimidated when you look at the bigness of our Savior: Jesus with his extravagant love, his reckless pursuit for justice, his staggering intelligence, his foolish bravery, his wisdom that confounds us all. In fact, God's extraordinary act of love—a deity taking on ordinary humanity for us—could be just as intimidating a picture of God as an exacting and angry tyrant.

So for a couple of days I wondered if there was something I was missing. How could a Jesus-looking God be more approachable and less scary than a tyrant God? What could keep the fear at bay—or at the very least, balance the two extremes?

Andrew, like me, is a big-picture, ambiance kind of person. When I stepped into the historic church building brought to life with this vibrant community of Jesus-followers, there was magic, comfort, love, and joy. The sanctuary had twinkling lights spread across the ceiling, which invited us to worship under a blanket of brilliance—magic.

Burlap and candles adorned the welcome table—comfort.

Pastries and coffee were available for early arrivals—love.

The introduction to Gungor's "Brother Moon" filled the room with xylophone, flute, and cello—joy.

While my husband got ready for the service, I sat in the second pew with my daughter, Trinity. She colored in her Hello Kitty coloring book while my boys, Tyson and T. J., created holy mischief under the black-and-white banners at the back of the sanctuary. I loved that they could made forts and hide under pews in this church, as I believe children should find the church a safe space for their imaginations. The world needs more imaginative theologians who can connect us to the heart of God in brave, new ways.

The tech guy turned on the preservice music, and Gungor began to play. Immediately, I pulled out my phone to look up the song in a song-recognition app called Shazam. (To this day, it's my most-used app. Say it with me: Shazam! Fun, right?)

Anyway, my daughter, who is incapable of staying still, suddenly jumped from the pew and started to dance in the aisle. With big curls and a bigger smile, Trinity danced with an enviable abandon to a lyric about how Jesus holds us together, how he makes everything new and everything beautiful. Watching my daughter dance, to these lyrics of the goodness of God, I knew it was time for my picture of God to be renewed.

I just sat there in our pew, a little happy and a little sad, and thought: Dance, baby, dance. Mama can't anymore. I'm too insecure. Too serious. Too afraid. So dance, baby, dance. You're safe and known here. Dance, baby, dance.

And she did. On her tippy-toes she twirled, and with arms outstretched, she bounced higher and higher to the beat. "Mama, come dance with me!" she squealed. And because it's impossible to deny a six-year-old, I jumped up. She laughed. Then I laughed. She danced. Then I danced.

Magic. Comfort. Love. Joy. All at once, dancing with my baby girl.

I'm not sure whether anybody saw us, and frankly, I'm not sure I care if they did. When the call to worship began, we returned to our seats—a little out of breath, a little giddy. As I caught my breath, the Holy Spirit reminded me of a time where I was sure God was good, loving, and kind.

* * *

When I was my daughter's age, while my mama and daddy talked on the porch. I'd take the rough concrete steps down to the soft carpet of grass, where I'd dance. There, under the Christmas lights my daddy left up in our trees because I begged him to, I'd dance with abandon. Bare feet pressing into the freshly watered grass, I was the girl who danced under the twinkly lights and Texas stars. My soul was satisfied. I knew I was safe. In that church in Providence, my daughter knew she was safe. So we danced.

In his book *Prototype*, Jonathan Martin recalls a word of encouragement from an elder in his church that his identity is more than that of pastor, writer, or leader. His identity, the elder told him, is that of "the boy on the bike." This encouragement reminded Martin of a Schwinn bike he loved as a kid. He would ride his bike for hours, making up dreams in his neighborhood cul-de-sac. He describes it as a sacred space where he was at home in his own skin, free of fear of God. As "the boy on the bike," he experienced the presence of God in a profound, real, deep, life-giving way. Riding his bike was not an explicitly spiritual practice, but it did teach him how to remain in the love of Jesus.

My confusion about God and his character as reflected in Jesus clicked into place as I embraced my invitation to be the girl who dances again. I had been afraid of God, but I had no reason to be. As the apostle Paul says in 1 John, reflecting on the love of God that holds all things together, "Perfect love casts out fear" (1 John 4:18 NRSV). And like Jonathan Martin, who found God on a bike, I wanted to find God as I dance.

Magic. Comfort. Love. Joy.

* * *

Jesus intimately knows the love of the Father and invites us into it when he teaches: "As the Father has loved me, so have I loved you. Now remain in my love" (John 15:9).

The Abba Father's love was sufficient to sustain Jesus for forty days in the wilderness and to comfort him through blood-punctuated prayers in Gethsemane. This love Jesus felt for us mobilized him to challenge oppressive authorities and walk the hill to Calvary. This love holds the kingdom of God together.

This perfect love invites us to be known and feel safe. Jesus' perfect love sets us free to be ourselves: hot messes, vulnerable, and broken—all this and more, yet still so deeply loved.

His is a love that has been ever present and ever flowing, for all time.

I was once told that if you want to have good theology about God and how he relates to us, then you should go back to the beginning. We should go to the garden of Eden, before the fall. Before sin. Before shame. Before brokenness. We should go back and examine how God and humankind related to one another.

In the garden, God breathed his very own life into us—an act so intimate the closest approximation we have is pregnancy. My blood became my children. My nourishment became theirs. My daughter has my eyes. My sons have my nose. You look at them and you see me. I look at them and I see me. This is the heart of God for us. God looks at us and sees himself, his precious creation.

In the garden, Adam and Eve were unguarded and unafraid. They made love without shame, cared for the ground without sweat, and walked in the cool of the evening with the divine. I kinda wanna say they danced naked under the pale moonlight too, because how can you not dance when all your needs are met? In the garden, Adam and Eve were at peace. They lived lives of shalom.

Then the Accuser came. Satan made Eve question God's integrity, his goodness, and his generosity. The serpent told Eve, "You surely will not die! For God knows that in the day you eat from it your eyes will be opened, and you will be like God, knowing good and evil" (Genesis 3:4-5 NASB).

With this one line, Satan handed the paintbrush of doubt to Eve. With it, she painted a picture of God as a self-serving tyrant and liar. Jesus came to redeem us not just from the sin that entered the world at the fall, but also from the picture of God that continually keeps us from finding shalom.

No matter whom I talk to, people are always trying to work their way back to Eden. They want the peace, flourishing, rest, and belonging of the garden. They want shalom. This is why certain metaphors—we're invited to sit at Jesus' table; we're invited to work alongside Jesus; we're on a journey with Jesus—resonate with so many of us. We simply want to belong and to know to whom we belong.

We were once separated from God, but because of Jesus, we are invited to remain in a love that sustains us, a love that reflects the kingdom of God, a love that empowers us to embody the kingdom of God right here on earth.

*   *   *

In my office, which is really half of Trinity's bedroom that she shares with me for work, there is a picture of a black ballerina in a pink tutu. The dancer's body has strokes of brown, cream, and tan. She is a representation of us all. Flowers of pink, white, and blue fall around her as if a doting fan has tossed them at her to celebrate her beauty. Wearing gorgeous mustard-yellow pointe shoes, she's in arabesque, with her arms joyfully above her head in third position. She looks as if she's about to leap or is just coming down from a leap. Either way, the vibrancy jumps off the picture. I want to step into the picture and dance with the ballerina. I look at this picture and think, "There's our Eden." We are invited into the circle dance of God's love, which transforms our hearts and brings our wholeness.

When a Shalom Sista says "I am invited," she is proclaiming a Jesus-looking picture of God that is more beautiful and more accessible than what religion or religious clichés would have us to believe. We say "We are invited" when we're afraid, because we know perfect love casts out fear. We are invited into a dance that encircles us with healing and hope. We dance because we know the God who has always loved us.

We dance, baby.

-5-

WOO-WOO CHURCH: WE ARE BELOVED

And now that you don't have to be perfect, you can be good.
—John Steinbeck

There is no perfect way to bring a child into the world. I learned this from having one baby at age twenty-one, another baby after a hurricane, and yet another baby just ten months later. Sometimes life throws us curveballs, and we find ourselves living a motherhood we did not imagine.

I was six years old when I found out that my parents had received one of these curveballs. Me. They didn't mean for me to find out that I was an "accident." But as we all know: kids are always listening. I was always listening—especially when my older half brother, whom I idolized, spoke.

At sixteen, my brother was flexing his muscles of independence. That day he wanted to go out with friends, but my dad had said no. My brother hadn't completed his chores, and my father didn't trust the friends. So they argued. I didn't know there was conflict when I went to offer my brother half my popsicle—you know, the kind that come as two stuck together. Those frozen delights were our first education in "sharing is caring." I had grabbed the last orange one, my brother's favorite flavor, and was going to offer him the other half. Standing in the hallway, I grew curious about the yelling. Then I heard my brother say, "You're always ruining my life, Dad. You're ruining it now by not letting me go out!"

Typical teen, right?

I reached for the doorknob to interrupt, but I stopped when I heard my brother yell my name.

"And you ruined my childhood when you left Mom for Osheta's mom! We were fine! We could have been happy, but then you left and took up with that woman! Why'd you go off and have a baby with her? Now you'll never get back with Mom. That little girl is the biggest mistake you've ever made. She came and she ruined everything for our family. I'll never forgive you for that!"

Silence filled the room. Outside the door, I held my breath. I had known that we had different mothers, but I hadn't known that my father had left his mother for mine. I didn't know that I was an accident.

Unexpected.

According to my brother, my father's biggest mistake.

I started to walk away from the door, but not before I heard my dad say, "It's true we didn't expect Osheta, but . . ." I don't remember anything else. I threw the popsicles away and ran outside. My world was turned upside down and I needed the safety of my swing.

Our backyard was my Eden. Don't ask me about the acreage, because math is hard, but I know there were at least four climbable trees that marked the four corners of our property. On the biggest tree, my dad had put up a swing. On the swing that day—the day I found out the circumstance of my birth—one word rocked in my soul with every push and pull. Mistake. Mistake. The biggest mistake. My brother's words played in my mind as my tears ran freely and the swing carried me up and down.

Up. ". . . biggest mistake."

Down. ". . . ruined everything."

Up. ". . . could have been happy."

Down. ". . . ruined our family."

Up. ". . . never forgive!"

I jumped off the swing and resolved to never be—or make—a mistake again. If by just existing I was a mistake, I would prove to my brother—and to the world—that I deserved to be here.

If I was a ferocious mistake, wasn't this the sensible thing to do? I just wanted my brother and dad to be happy and get along. Even as child I was attempting to be a peacemaker in all the wrong ways. Of course these were illogical thoughts, but what six-year-old thinks clearly?

This was the nexus of my shame and perfectionism. This is the problem with being a peacemaker before you yourself are whole: you absorb pain and release heartache.

I come from a proud Texas town surrounded by oil refineries and fueled by Friday night football. I began begging my parents to take me along to my brother's football games so that I could cheer him on. How could he hate his loudest, cutest cheerleader? Fairly easily, I guess, because when I attended his games, he paid little, if any, attention to me. But perfectionism doesn't give up. It simply finds new ways to latch on to significance. I would come home from his games and frost store-bought sugar cookies with icing, then affix M&M's in his school's colors on them. Before going to bed, I'd leave a plate of orange and black cookies on his desk. The next day, the plate would be empty—come on, y'all, he was a teenager. But he never said thank you.

I was a teenager by the time I worked up the courage to tell my dad what I heard in the hallway and the impact it had on me. The moment after he heard this was one of the few times I've seen my dad cry. He never wanted me to feel unloved and unwanted.

I was never called a mistake again, mind you. My brother never brought it up with me. But I still deeply felt the impact of his words that day. In fact, they've stayed with me all my life.

It only takes one time, doesn't it? One time being called a nag. One time being called lazy, or ugly, or fat, or unwanted. One time is all it takes for a careless word to latch on to your soul like a tick and suck away your identity. That one time fuels an endless cycle of self-hate that, if not stopped, will crush our spirits.

Sweet Sista, what words have you attached to your soul that try to limit your identity and force you to live with shame? What are the things you tell yourself that you would never say to your worst enemy? When you look at yourself in the mirror, who do you say that you are?

Our hearts break when we believe we are not wanted and have no place in this world. In the kingdom of God, we remain in God's love. We are beloved.

It would be a long time until I learned this.

✳ ✳ ✳

Years later, with my newborn daughter sleeping peacefully in my lap, I thought of that day my brother called me a mistake. From the outside, the scene may have looked tranquil and maternal, but I was completely broken inside. "I made a mistake," I whispered under my breath. My daughter was so trusting, and I was so unhinged. I did not think I was capable of being perfect anymore.

On paper, I rocked that year after Katrina. I was the Katrina survivor, the supermom of three little kids, the supportive wife, and the interesting former urban missionary. My husband was at work during day and at school in the evening, and I was managing everything. The acquaintances I made in our new church in Boston celebrated me for my courage. How could I tell them that I was floundering? Everyone needed me to hold it together.

In truth, I was exhausted from giving birth twice in one year and overwhelmed with living in a new place, and I felt so alone so much of the time. I didn't know it at the time, but I was also suffering from acute postpartum depression. All I knew was that deep down inside, I believed I was just a mistake: a mistake who had made a mistake by having another baby.

With my baby sleeping in my lap and my soul suffocating from depression, I made a horrible decision. Since I should not have been here in the first place, I would fix my parents' mistake and take myself out of the equation altogether.

I laid my daughter down in the room where her brothers were napping, turned on the water in the bathtub, and went to the kitchen to find a knife. I was behind on washing the dishes, which angered me even more. How pathetic, I thought to myself; I can't even find a clean knife to take my own life! Eventually I found a paring knife that seemed appropriate and clean enough. I checked on the kids once more, kissed their sweet faces for what I thought would be the last time, and went to the bathroom to disrobe.

I had a short window of time before T. C. came home from work to change and then go to school, so I wanted to get it over with quickly. Thankfully, I wasn't quick enough. He came home and found me on the bathroom floor, weeping, with the paring knife to my wrist.

The thing about nearly taking your life is that later, when you try to remember, it's all a blur, really.

I remember the yelling and the crying.

I remember my husband holding me, and the clatter of the knife hitting the linoleum floor.

I remember one word still throbbing in my brain. Mistake.

*　*　*

I am the product of a second marriage, which left me questioning if God had erred in breathing life into my mama's womb. I am the darkest child of four. With my mocha skin, I've always felt ugly compared to my Irish cream mama and my cappuccino sisters. I am smart but often confused, so too often the words I say and the words I mean aren't the same thing. I am the person whose name is never pronounced right, which puts me in the awkward position of correcting new friends.

And I am the woman who, once upon a time, wanted to die.

In the days after T. C. found me in the bathroom, I was put on antidepressants for postpartum depression. I started therapy for post-traumatic stress. Gradually, I began to feel better; each day was no longer a dull gray pit of despair.

Things began looking up, except for one thing. I did everything right, and yet the word *mistake* played like a ticker tape in my mind.

I think this is why, during that season of life, I said "I'm sorry" for small infractions nearly every day. I'd forget to hold the door for someone and say, "I'm sorry." I'd interrupt employees at the grocery store to ask a question and start by saying, "I'm sorry!" When I wasn't "in the mood" because I had been "touched out" by three little ones, "I'm so, so sorry, babes. Tomorrow, I promise."

At the same time, I lived with a need to prove my competence. I volunteered and led small groups. I quoted obscure theologians. Hard vocabulary words became my liturgy, and compliments from other people—"Wow, I'm so impressed with you!"—became my benediction. I built my identity with the false gold of praise and responsibilities. Daily I worshiped at the altar of perfectionism.

There's a story in the Bible about idols and God's love that I often think of when I reflect on my season of perfectionism. Paul was walking around Athens one time when he noticed that the Athenians were earnest in their faith but were misguided by the lure of perfectionism. They wanted to get the whole "religion" thing right, so they built idols to every single god—even to one called an unknown god. I imagine the residents looking around and thinking, "Let's just cover all our bases so that when the time comes, we can say, 'We were competent, faithful, and wise. We did not make a single mistake.'"

I could relate. But Paul, knowing Jesus and having experienced the transformative power of the love of God in his own life, was grieved by the Athenians' idol worship. There was so much more for them. Paul stood up to tell them about how he was turned upside down from a rule-follower to a Jesus-follower. He preached to those people who just wanted to get it right and told them that the very God who created the heavens and the earth—the God who breathed life into their bodies and who stood before history and time—wanted to be close to them that very moment. "In him we live and move and have our being" (Acts 17:28), Paul told them, borrowing the words of Epimenides, a popular philosopher-poet.

In whom do you, Sista, live and move and have your being? Whom do you let define you? Who calls you their own?

The more I studied shalom, the more I noticed the emphasis on God's love as our foundation for identity. God is love, and his love holds all things together. In that love, we live wholeheartedly, move with confidence, and are called beloved. The kingdom of God is sustained by the love of God, and a Shalom Sista knows that. We look to Jesus to show us how to resist the culture of "Try harder, be better, prove your worth" that comes to challenge this resolve. Once we know who we truly are, we can love the Lord with all our hearts, with no reservations, and with no shame holding us back.

We are beloved. I had to learn this, slowly. And I did. But first, I had to have a baptism.

✳ ✳ ✳

The church we attended in Cambridge was your textbook definition of a "woo-woo" church. The people there talked to Jesus as if he were sitting across from them, cross-legged, on his own bohemian throw pillow. When they prayed, they'd mention the pictures the Spirit was giving them for guidance. They had artists on the stage to draw while the pastor preached. They raffled off those pieces and gave the money to the poor. They danced in the aisles with ribbons and tambourines, and they even had a deliverance ministry. They were very in touch with their emotions. For Jesus.

Now. I came to faith in a Pentecostal church. I can whoop and holler and shame the devil with the best of them. My favorite shirt right now is one that says "Not today, Satan," and I wear it often. When my teenage son acts a fool, I just point to my shirt. If Jesus could rebuke his disciples, I figure I can rebuke a hormonal teen. Trust me. Woo-woo does not scare me.

Vulnerability, though? That terrifies me to the core. And that's what I saw in these Jesus-lovers: a vulnerability to God. I wasn't sure I could handle that.

To claim our true identity, we have to strip away our defenses—our false identity. Those false identities are like armor with holes and missing pieces, leaving us vulnerable and unprotected. God's love, though, is a solid breastplate of righteousness. (And I know, girl . . . I roll my eyes too when my friends start quoting the armor of God at me. But hear me out.) We don't receive the righteousness that brings our shalom because we worked for it and got it right. There are no hustle buses in the kingdom of God. Righteousness is standing tall because we are already right. Already accepted. Already loved and valued just because we exist. Belovedness requires a vulnerability that says "I am worthy because I am." Nothing more. Nothing else.

This is the worst thing to ask a perfectionist to accept, which is why Woo-Woo Church annoyed the heck out of me.

On my last official day of therapy, my counselor suggested I join a support group. And guess what joke God pulled on me. One of the support groups my therapist suggested—the one designed for people healing from past hurts—was hosted by none other than Woo-Woo Church.

This six-week support group was called Living Streams in the Desert. (I mean, just typing that makes me feel too woo-woo to function, but let's just press on.) The deal was this: if you had someone willing to sponsor you and meet with you at the beginning and end of the program, then you could join.

I did not want my perfectionism to drive me back to the bathroom floor, so I reached out to the organizer. She told me that someone I already knew was a sponsor looking for a participant.

Carolyn was the leader of a small group for moms that I had visited a few times before I had Trinity, before the postpartum depression set in, before the bathroom floor. I was scared to share this piece of my story with her, because I wanted Carolyn to like me. She is one of the most balanced women I've ever met. She's gorgeous but kind. Generous but wise. Eager but thoughtful.

When I visited Carolyn to talk about the Living Streams support group, she greeted me at the door in a T-shirt and holey yoga pants. I don't mean, like, trendy holey yoga pants, because those are actually a thing you can buy now. No, dear reader, I mean the kind you love so much because they're just the right length so that they don't drag on the ground, even when you rock your Chucks with them. Also, your bum looks amazing in them—every single time you wear them. Life lesson, Sistas: you be good and faithful to any pair of pants that give you bum confidence. Take Carolyn's example: do not throw them out, and own that confidence by greeting your protégé at the door in them.

Carolyn the Confident met me at the door in her holey yoga pants, and my whole life changed. We walked through the application together, and she spoke to my fears of not being "spiritual" enough for the class. "This is about you and Jesus, Osheta," she said. "Don't worry about anyone else. You are there for your healing."

She put down her mug of Trader Joe's chai and took my hands in hers. Looking deeply into my eyes, she asked one question: "What do you want Jesus to do?"

Jesus once asked a similar question during his ministry. He asked this question to a blind man, Bartimaeus, who replied, "Rabbi, I want to see." I wanted to see too. I wanted my eyes to be opened to see myself as God sees me. Everyone around me spoke of this belovedness, but I didn't believe it for myself. So I shrugged and answered Carolyn: "I want to believe that God really loves me."

With a knowing look in her eyes, Carolyn said, "Let's pray and ask Jesus to give you a picture."

As Carolyn prayed for me, she asked God to help me come out different, whole, and feeling loved. I didn't get a picture, but I did get one phrase. I prayed this phrase the whole six weeks: "Lord, let me be baptized in your love."

* * *

In Matthew, there is a story about Jesus before he performed a single miracle, before he taught a moving parable, and before he walked to Calvary. This story is foundational for us as we seek shalom in our relationship with God.

> Then Jesus arrived from Galilee at the Jordan coming to John, to be baptized by him. But John tried to prevent Him, saying, "I have need to be baptized by You, and do You come to me?" But Jesus answering said to him, "Permit it at this time; for in this way it is fitting for us to fulfill all righteousness." Then he permitted Him. After being baptized, Jesus came up immediately from the water; and behold, the heavens were opened, and he saw the Spirit of God descending as a dove and lighting on Him, and behold, a voice out of the heavens said, "This is My beloved Son, in whom I am well-pleased." (Matthew 3:13-17 NASB)

Imagine with me: Jesus, walking up to the river Jordan where John the Baptist was baptizing people. This, in and of itself, was a revolutionary act. The Israelites had crossed over into the Promised Land through the river Jordan. It symbolized a new journey into a new promised land. At the same time, purification by water was solely done in the temple—not in a river, where anyone could access wholeness. Yet John knew that when the Messiah came, he would come to cleanse and restore all people. So he baptized in the wilderness, where anyone and everyone could come, repent, and be made whole. It was one of John's protests against the corruption of the world. This is where Jesus began his ministry of revealing the heart of God to us. Here, by the river Jordan, Jesus staged a protest and a promise.

Perfect Jesus. Our Jesus, who had nothing to repent of, knew his identity as God's Son from childhood. Yet it was important for him to step in line to identify with us. I believe he knew what was going happen when he came up from the water. I believe he knew he was going to be called beloved: a Son loved by the Creator of the heavens and earth. That one identity was for him—and for every single person who follows him.

You see, Jesus didn't do anything to be able to be called beloved. Remember, this was at the beginning of his ministry. Jesus wasn't even from an ideal family. He didn't have the ideal or even expected birth story. No. Jesus, just as himself, was precious and loved by God.

Sista, you and I, just as ourselves, are precious and loved by God.

This assurance is what we build our shalom practices on. If we as women know that we are loved, no matter what, then that love casts out all fear. That love casts out all terror of God, of loving our enemies, or of speaking truth to those who oppress the weak. That love makes us want to share our resources. That love might even make us step into a woo-woo church and feel all vulnerable and tender.

When we hear the Spirit whisper to us of our belovedness, we are empowered to pray for ourselves, for our families, for our communities, for our world. After all, we are beloved, and Abba Father hears our cries.

God's love holds us together when we grieve, and it galvanizes our resolve to walk gently in a violent world. We know we are not alone or forgotten.

Baptism is one of the most important sacraments for a Christian. It's more than ritual; it's a claiming of our true identity among our new family. It's both a personal and communal declaration that we are kingdom people. The candidate goes down into the water one way and comes up another. Maybe when she steps into the baptismal water she hears the lies of the world that say she's a slut, or a failure, or a flake, or a mistake. Those lies desperately attempt to cling to her. But she knows that in the waters of baptism, the love of God will rinse them away. She stands before her spiritual siblings, vulnerable and brave, tender and ready. She makes a vow to denounce the lies of Satan and the forces of evil in this world. The celebrant lowers her into the water and brings her back up anew. The first thing a new believer hears as she comes out of the water is the raucous celebration of fellow beloveds. Baptism is for the new believer and community alike. As we celebrate her belovedness, we remember ours.

Practically speaking, we can't get baptized every Sunday. I know that desire to reenter the joy of baptism well—growing up,

I was notorious for getting saved and baptized at every vacation Bible school, revival meeting, and summer camp. We can, however, be baptized in the love of God every single day. We can start by claiming that we are beloved.

When I look in the mirror and my hair is a hot mess . . . I am beloved.

When I snap at my daughter because I haven't had my coffee (and let me tell you, the force of sass is strong with that one) . . . I am beloved.

When I forget to pay a bill and I get the annoying robocall reminder . . . I am beloved.

When I'm going about my day and I feel alone . . . I am beloved.

Through every circumstance, when I am aware of the forces of this world pressing in with the words *mistake*, *bad*, *wrong*, or *unwanted*, I stop. I remember Jesus. I think about what he said to Nicodemus, a Pharisee who wondered what it takes for a person to be born again. Jesus had just told him that no one can see the kingdom of God unless they are born again. This stumped Nicodemus. He was grown man, unsure of how to replicate birth or restore innocence. Jesus responded, "Very truly I tell you, no one can enter the kingdom of God unless they are born of water and the Spirit" (John 3:5).

Water and Spirit. May the water of God's love wash away every false identity you hold. May the Spirit alight on you with your new name: Beloved.

There is no perfect way to bring a child into this world. I have accepted my birth because I see the love of God. I stand with arms wide open and feel the warmth of God's affection on my chest and I say, "I am beloved." Saying this is like breathing in oxygen. I breathe in God's pleasure, and I breathe out the shame.

Again and again, I breathe in God's love and I breathe out shame until I am made whole.

-6-

Coffee Shop Alias: We Are Enough

We do not need magic to transform the world. We carry all the power we need inside ourselves already.
—J. K. Rowling

When we meet, I will take you out for coffee. But before we sit down to share our hearts and cheer each other on as peacemakers, you're gonna see me do something a little strange. I don't want you to be alarmed. When the barista goes to take my order and asks me what name she should write on the cup, I am not going to say Osheta.

With a name like mine, I have confused, annoyed, and surprised many people. In fact, there are three common responses to my name.

Confusion: Wait . . . what? How do you spell that?

Me: O-S-H-E-T-A. The *t* sounds like a *d*, so it always throws people off.

Curiosity: Wow, I've never heard that before. What does it mean?

Me: Nothing. My dad made it up when he was in Okinawa during the Vietnam War. He liked the sound of the Japanese language and he always wanted a daughter, so when my mom told him she was having a girl, he immediately knew my name: Osheta.

Condescension: How exotic! How interesting! I've never heard that name! I wish I had a cool name like that! You must have a hard time finding personalized items, huh?

Me: Yeah. Just don't try to buy me a keychain from a roadside gas station and we're good.

Most of the time, people compliment me and say that my name is beautiful, and I agree, even though it's just not an easy name to learn. In her poem "Difficult Names," poet Warsan Shire says to give your daughters difficult names, for in those names their characters are refined and their instincts will be honed. This is true.

Because of my name, I used to plan to show up late for coffee dates. I'd ask my friend to order for me, then pay her in cash when I showed up. All this just so I wouldn't have to do the whole name-on-your-cup routine. If I held up the line with spelling my name or saying it several times for the barista, I noticed the customers behind me start to show signs of impatience—excessive phone swiping, fingers-on-hips tapping, throat clearing.

But I've found the solution: a coffee shop alias.

It all started when I sent my son into Starbucks to get me a coffee and he asked the barista to write "Tyson is the coolest" on my coffee cup. That kid giggled every time I took a drink. Impish little guy. When I shared the cup on Instagram, I captioned it that maybe my son was onto something, since I never want to tell the barista my name because it's so different. In the comments, my friend James challenged me to go to Starbucks for a whole week and every day tell them a new pop star diva's name—and share pics, of course. Nothing is official until you share it online, right?

I took him up on that challenge—until my husband told me that seven days' worth of Starbucks was out of the question. I could go three times, so I had to choose three divas wisely.

Monday, I was Mariah.

Tuesday, I was our girl Janet.

And Friday, on our date night, I was Whitney.

Whitney stuck.

It's my maiden name, so I easily recognize it when it is yelled above the indie pop soundtrack and hissing espresso machines. Plus, like Whitney, I almost always wanna dance with somebody.

So when we go to coffee, friend, I'll be on time. I'll pay for both of us, even if you order something weird like a matcha latte. To the barista, I'll go by Whitney. You can still call me Osheta, though. My given name, Osheta, reminds me of my father's love and his delight. My alias, Whitney, is a "middle" name of sorts—it gives me confidence and ease as I move through a world that has little patience for unique names.

The same is true for our spiritual names. If Beloved is our first name, given to us by God to bring wholeness to our identities, then Enough is our middle name, revealing God's dream for us to live out our belovedness in a world that will always ask us to prove it. Beloved and Enough are two sides of the same coin of identity. One faces God: "I know you call me Beloved." The other faces the world: "God calls me Beloved, so I am Enough."

* * *

In addition to having clichés, Christian subculture has got some go-to sayings. They are folksy, and they help pastors drive home their point from the pulpit. Sometimes they are helpful and sometimes they are not. Among these are "Too blessed to be stressed" and "God is good all the time; all the time God is good."

As I began to explore traditions different from the one in which I came to faith, I slowly stopped using these sayings in my everyday life, save for one: "You cannot live on mountaintop experiences alone." Variations include: "You can't live for Sunday only. You've gotta take Sunday right into your Monday"; or if you're in a youth group: "You can't live at camp; you've gotta take camp back home with you."

I was fifteen the first time I heard this mountaintop phrase used in church. We had a particularly moving church service, and before we left, our pastor stood up and said, "Tonight was a mountaintop experience, friends. In unique ways we were all touched by the Lord. Like Moses on the mountaintop, who saw God move and it changed his life. But here's the thing." She threw her Bible down and leaned over the podium. (Church pro tip: if your pastor leans over the podium after throwing down her Bible, you better listen, Sista.) "Moses went back down to the Israelites and his life with his people. You cannot live on mountaintop experiences alone. You have to go back into the valleys of your everyday life and take the mountaintop with you." Sometimes *wilderness* is substituted for *valleys*, but you get the point.

Full disclosure: I used to get so irritated with Jesus' time in the wilderness. (See Matthew 4 for the story of the temptations.) Jesus had just been baptized, which was this amazing moment for his ministry. Everyone saw not just Jesus, the Messiah whom John the Baptist had been preaching about for years. They saw the Holy Spirit come down like a dove, and heard the Father audibly speak. Audibly *speak*, y'all. Why wouldn't Jesus have capitalized on that moment? Shouldn't he have stayed with the crowds and taught more about what had just happened? I mean, he had a captive audience. Talk about a mountaintop experience!

But what happened in the wilderness is vital for us if we want to experience the shalom of God in our identities. In the wilderness, Jesus rejected the tyranny of "if only" that challenges our belief that we are enough. I've suffered under this tyranny more than a few times. "If only my kids were more well-behaved, then . . ." or "If only I was a few sizes smaller, then . . ." or "If only I had a few more followers on Twitter." "If only" is always followed by some qualifier that we think will validate our worth and bestow our belovedness. A Shalom Sista summarily rejects "if only."

No "if only," already. We are already Beloved because we are Enough.

We are baptized as Beloved on the mountaintop, and Enough is what we take down into the valleys. These names work in tandem to create our wholeness.

Our culture loves its metrics and standards. We, being immersed in this culture, judge ourselves by numbers on a scale, letters behind our names, or dollars in our bank accounts. We measure our importance by the amount of time it takes our friends to text us back. If those dancing dots don't pop up immediately, we worry, "Do they love me? Did I do something wrong? Maybe I shouldn't have texted them in the first place."

It's a demoralizing way to live, don't you think?

It's so easy to forget that Jesus did nothing to earn his beloved-ness or to justify that he was Jesus. There are days when I want to believe I am beloved, but I know my sins and I know the hurtful words I carelessly speak. Honestly, there are days when I feel more bespeckled than beloved. As I judge myself by the standard of "Do more, be better, get it done, and never make a mistake," I can feel the light of the mountaintop waning in my soul and I'm left shivering in the cold in the valley.

So what do I do with that?

For most of us, assuming our new identity as Beloved poses a problem. We feel like imposters because we didn't earn our belovedness, or we can't easily prove it. When we use these same metrics and measurements for our relationships with God, we are in a constant struggle to secure or qualify our belovedness. "If only I . . ." becomes our running narrative. "If only I read the Bible more, worshiped more freely, or joined the right small group. If only, if only, if only . . ." The list goes on and on. Our creativity knows no bounds when it comes to diminishing our own worth.

Psychologists have a term for this experience: imposterism. Poet Maya Angelou once said, "Each time I write a book, every time I face that yellow pad, the challenge is so great. I have written eleven books, but each time I think, 'Uh oh, they're going to find out now. I've run a game on everybody and they're going to find me out.'" If even Maya Angelou still feels like an imposter, is there any hope for the rest of us?

Social psychologist Amy Cuddy identifies imposterism as "the deep and sometimes paralyzing belief that we have been given something we didn't earn and don't deserve and that at some point we'll be exposed." In a TED talk, Cuddy recounts a life-threatening car accident in which she sustained a brain injury that prevented her from processing information. Because of her injury, she lost IQ points and brain functionality, and she could not return to college. She confesses that it was as if her core identity had been taken away from her.

After years of hard work, Cuddy finally finished college and even entered grad school at Princeton. But still she felt that she did not belong in the Ivy League. Deep down, she felt that she hadn't earned the honor, and therefore she didn't deserve it. Ultimately, she thought, she had fooled everyone.

She began studying the mind and body connection and came across an interesting hack to insecurity and imposterism: power poses.

Her TED talk is often referred to as the "Superman stance" talk, because in it Cuddy talks about power poses: expansive, open, space-occupying postures that can actually affect how we feel about ourselves and increase confidence in nerve-racking situations. When we feel like imposters, choosing a confident posture in the world can help us move more freely and act more boldly.

We are enough. This is a Shalom Sista's power pose. This is the posture that emboldens her to live wholeheartedly in a broken-hearted world.

This manifesto point—We are enough—creates a whole new metric that qualifies our belovedness with God's unconditional love for us. It's us living into the security of the kingdom of God where we are called sons and daughters. There is a Scripture that I love to say when I'm feeling unsure of my belovedness: "We love because he first loved us" (1 John 4:19). Enough gives me the courage I need to love myself. Enough keeps the fire of God's delight burning bright in my heart.

Enough is the embodiment of my belovedness. It puts actions to my beliefs. Like Maya Angelou, every day we wake up with the fear of being found out. Our days are like blank yellow pads. Every day we're challenged to write a better story about our identity, a story that rejects the fear that we're going to be exposed to others or that God is going rescind our belovedness.

I had to remind myself I was enough when I got invited to a swanky Hollywood luncheon.

*   *   *

As a general rule, I don't reply to messages on Facebook. Anybody and everybody can message you, which means if my high school boyfriend Shane wanted to look me up to ask if he can stay with us in Los Angeles while he auditions for *Days of Our Lives*, he could. Then I'd spend hours stressing out over the inevitable no I'd have to give him, partly because meeting up with high school exes anywhere but a high school reunion is pretty much a terrible idea. But also, he really wasn't that great an actor in high school.

This is why I nearly missed a message from Jessica, the CEO of a fair trade accessory company in Austin, Texas, that I love. Her company empowers businesswomen here in America to create a marketplace for talented artisans in developing countries, thereby helping them rise out of poverty. I was actually searching for a message from a potential podcast guest that had gotten lost in the mix when I saw this short message: "Hey Osheta! It's Jessica. I have a question to ask you. Here's my cell phone number; shoot me a text."

That's it.

I almost thought her account must have been hacked, because preteens with too much time on their hands and a working of knowledge of coding are a real thing these days. But I decided to text her anyway. "Hey Jessica. It's Osheta. I got your Facebook message . . . what's up?"

"Hey girl!" her reply began, and my nerves settled. This was definitely Jessica—I knew because she had invoked the customary Texan girl greeting "Hey girl." Thank goodness it wasn't Shane using his bratty nephew's hacking skills to get at me and trick me into saying yes to his request to crash on my couch for his audition. (Did I mention things did not end well with Shane and me? They rarely do when you date a thespian.) Nope, it wasn't Shane. It was the cofounder of one of my favorite companies in the world texting me back.

Jessica went on to ask me if I was still in Los Angeles, if I was still a supporter of her company, and if I'd seen the new line of jewelry yet.

Yes, yes, and yes, I texted back.

Big, pretty earrings are my love language.

The dancing dots popped up on the screen, and I fidgeted in my seat. What was all this about? I knew Jessica was a very busy woman running a multimillion dollar company with connections in more than eleven countries. I couldn't imagine her randomly texting people in the middle of the day. Did she want me to host a trunk show in Los Angeles? Was she in town and needing a pickup at the airport? Wait! Had Shonda Rhimes called and asked for someone to help her pick out some pieces for a red-carpet appearance and I immediately came to mind when Jessica and her team thought, "Who loves *Grey's Anatomy* and great big earrings?"

"Perfect!" she replied. "I was wondering if you'd come and speak to a group of women I'm gathering to share the new line. I'm speaking, but I want you to share your story and why you support the company. Are you in?"

I waited for a beat.

"There's a lot of details; I'm sending you an email right now. Let me know what you think."

When the email came, it was an invitation to a luncheon at a swanky Hollywood restaurant. At the moment I received it, I was the furthest thing from stylish. My hair was in a bun on top of my head, kinda ratty because I had gone swimming the night before and black women's hair does not bounce back well from chlorine. My favorite yoga pants had a huge paint stain on the bum. I was wearing the camisole top to a pajama set that I had lost the bottoms to, and my nails were chipping. Oh, and did I mention the luncheon was in four days?

I knew I had some time to clean up, but then I started thinking about the caliber of women in that group. When Jessica told me the names of some of the women they had invited, I stupidly checked out their Instagram accounts. One of them hosted a styling school. A twentysomething beauty with perfect red lipstick had over two hundred thousand followers. And in just a few weeks, I was going to begin work as an intern for another.

To say I didn't think I fit in is an understatement.

Actual conversations between the hubs and me about the swanky luncheon:

Day 1

Me: There's this thing in Hollywood that I have to go speak at.

T. C.: That's great, babers. You're going to kill it.

Me: Well . . . I think I need a new outfit.

T. C.: Well . . . then buy a new outfit.

Me: Well . . . I just paid the electricity bill, so we have forty-three dollars left in the account.

T. C.: Find something in your closet.

Day 2

Me: I have nothing to wear to this Hollywood thing. I hate Hollywood and beautiful people and swanky restaurants with chandeliers and reclaimed wood. That just ups the freaking clothes ante. I. Can't. Do. This! [Falls on a pile of clothes.]

T. C.: What about that red long dress you wear sometimes?

Me: Eww, no! Too springy. Babes, it's a sleeveless maxi.

T. C.: There's that black thing with the straps.

Me: You mean the A-line sundress?

T. C.: Whatever. You look good in that.

Me: Are you not understanding that this is a "fall line," so I need to wear fall-ish colors?

T. C.: What's a fall color? Orange? That red dress has some orange in it—

Me: [Throws a hanger.] Get out.

Day 3

Me: Your paycheck hit the account! I'm going to Goodwill!

T. C.: So . . . you're going to find something "swanky luncheon speaker" appropriate at Goodwill?

Me: Around here, yes! These suburban LA women donate the best things. Kate Spade, holla!

T. C.: Okay, well . . . whatever that means. Have fun, babers, and treat yourself to some shoes.

Me: It's cute that you thought you had to give me permission to buy shoes.

* * *

I did find a dress at Goodwill, and I did buy shoes. I borrowed some pieces from the new line from someone I knew who sold the jewelry, and I was all set. All the right pieces were in place. My hair was no longer a rat's nest. I loved my new (to me) dress. T. C. approved of the shoes.

The morning of the luncheon, I worked on my talk with the deep sense that I was missing an opportunity to practice shalom for myself. "Not enough, not enough, not enough" was the phrase I thought repeatedly from the moment Jessica invited me to speak.

I worried that I wasn't enough. Smart enough. Stylish enough. Pretty enough. Had enough followers. Knew enough about the pieces or the artisan groups that created them.

I kept thinking back to the Instagram accounts. How put together and lovely those women were. I thought about my last-season Kate Spade dress and imagined someone walking in wearing something from the current season and knowing that I was an imposter. I liked to imagine I had something important to say. But when you got right down to it, I was just a girl in a dress from Goodwill.

I flurried around the house looking for earrings, shoes, and lipstick, my head so full of notes and noise that I couldn't listen to the leading of the Holy Spirit. If I had listened, the Spirit would have been telling me that I was enough, but I didn't want to accept it. I felt too vulnerable to accept that no matter what happened that afternoon, to God, I was beloved, and therefore I was enough.

On the drive to Hollywood, I prayed for the luncheon. I knew Jessica was a believer too, so I prayed for her and the attendees. I prayed for their anxieties, and I prayed for really great conversation around the table. I prayed for myself to get over my anxiety and really be present.

I really need to be careful what I pray for.

I spoke. I think I was pretty good. Speaking is one of my favorite things to do. Unlike some people, I don't get stage fright. I get this sense of clarity and calm. Oftentimes, when I'm speaking to a group, I realize I'm actually speaking to myself, and this day was no exception. I told the women about how much I loved the company, about how partnering with the company gave me a sense of purpose in the global poverty crisis. I told them how empowered I felt in helping our family make ends meet when I sold the jewelry as an ambassador , and most of all, how I loved that Jessica surrounds herself with authentic women who want to do good in the world with whatever is in their hands.

When I sat down, the woman across from me, Krista, smiled at me and said, "I just loved what you said up there."

I thanked her and reached for my water glass with my right hand. Krista gasped as she caught a glimpse of my dove tattoo. "That's a really cool tattoo," she said. "I think doves are so pretty."

"Thanks," I said. "I got it because I love peacemaking and I'm a person of faith. It reminds me of when Jesus was called beloved at his baptism and how God thinks I'm beloved too."

"Stop!" She raised her wrist. There, in a tiny script, was the word *beloved* in lowercase. "*Beloved* was a really important thing for me when I started my business," Krista said. "It's so easy for me to get caught up in the number of likes and followers I have. This tattoo reminds me I'm beloved without any of that."

I didn't have anything to say. I was a woman wearing a tattoo with a very similar meaning, yet I didn't own my belovedness. I still thought I was not enough.

*　*　*

In the days after the luncheon, I thought about Jesus in the desert, owning his belovedness. With every option Satan offered—turn these stones to bread, throw yourself off the temple, bow down and worship me—Jesus had a choice. He could believe the lie of scarcity—you don't have enough, so you cannot truly be beloved; you must do something to prove it—or he could believe the truth of abundance.

I thought about the very literal metaphor of the desert, which by its very nature is a scarce, barren, and dry place. Maybe this was exactly the right place for the Spirit to lead Jesus so that he could be tempted by Satan.

It's quite possible that we who are saturated with stuff and ideas and opportunities need to read this story and be amazed at the confidence of Jesus in a scarce place. Jesus overcame the scarcity thinking of "I'm not enough" by trusting in the abundance of the kingdom of God. In every instance in which Jesus could have fashioned his own solution, he rejected the temptation and chose to trust God.

Like Jesus, we are enough, and we have enough, because we have God.

I wonder if, during his ministry, Jesus thought back to his time in the desert and how he relied on the abundance, the wellspring of living water, and the daily bread found in his relationship with the Father. Sometimes, when I don't feel that I'm enough and I'm questioning my belovedness, I think that I must be missing something—a mountaintop experience, an awesome retreat, the latest worship album.

But I'm learning that we cannot match the abundance of the kingdom with earthly stuff. When I'm tempted to look to my phone for connection, my closet for validation, and my bank account for protection, I have to stop and say, "I am beloved, and I am enough."

Two spiritual names flesh out our kingdom identity. God calls us Beloved; therefore, we are Enough.

Part III

Shalom within Ourselves

-1-

THIS BROWN SKIN: WE WILL SEE THE BEAUTY

And i said to my body. softly. "i want to be your friend." it took a long breath. and replied "i have been waiting my whole life for this."
—Nayyirah Waheed

I hope you don't mind me telling you this, but I think you're beautiful." The white boy who blocked my exit from the pew had tidepool blue eyes. I noticed specks of gray in them as he leaned in close—I guess to make sure I heard him over the worship band playing for the altar call. I looked around the room for confirmation that yes, in fact, this total stranger had just given me probably the sweetest, most self-assured pickup line ever.

The college chapel was filled with young adults on fire for the Lord. During my sophomore year in college, the young adults at my church in Texas decided to give up our spring break to do urban ministry. Our denomination supported a practical, hands-on Bible college that hosted short-term mission trips to raise awareness and recruit students. Our pastor pitched it to us as a chance to be "light in a dark city during one of its darkest events": Mardi Gras.

If you had asked me why I signed up for the trip, I would have had no virtuous reason. It was peer pressure. I had no desire to visit New Orleans. I vaguely knew about Mardi Gras because Galveston, a city twenty minutes from my hometown, hosts a mini version of Mardi Gras on Fat Tuesday. But that was pretty much the extent of my knowledge. Still, twentysomething Christian women are incapable of missing an opportunity to meet new, available, and missional Christian men, so we sign up for crazy things like laser tag, wilderness weekends, and mission trips to cities of debauchery.

Now the boy was waiting expectantly for my response, and I needed a minute to collect myself. He was altogether too forward and clearly going about Christian dating all wrong. Everyone knows that Christian boys first show off with their Bible knowledge, then they play with some kids, and then they strum "I Exalt Thee" (terribly) on the guitar. Only after this trifecta of holy hotness are they allowed to approach you. Bold Boy did none of these. He just walked up to me and started talking. I was scandalized and a little annoyed at his rebellion against the rules. Man, if only I had known what was in store for me over the next sixteen years, I would have saved my indignation.

I looked around the room one more time for help. Surely someone's spiritual spidey sense should have tingled a warning: "Potential boy-girl impropriety here! Must douse this young love with holy water or foil it with a shame-filled stare!"

But no one heard him. What with the band singing "I Surrender All" for the umpteenth time—this time in a higher octave so that we would all feel the urgency—I really couldn't blame them. I was left alone to deal with the bold boy.

"Oh, okay . . ." I drew out my response, holding my Bible closer to me. If my purity comrades were not coming to my aid, I could go old school and keep at least a Bible's width between us. He leaned back and smiled. I faltered a bit, said "Thanks!" and side-stepped him into the aisle to make my way out of the chapel.

He watched me walk away. I know this because, as if in a cliché rom-com meet cute, I turned around to look. There he was, looking all rebel without a cause and confident. He shrugged and sat in the pew I had just vacated.

Face hot and heart beating, I ran to the dorm room where I was staying for the week. My best friend Jamie was gathering her shower supplies when I came in.

"Heeeeeyy!" she singsonged. She put down her shower caddy and grabbed my hands excitedly. "I saw that guy head over to you. What did he say?"

Traitor, I thought. The least she could have done was stay with me. Maybe the boy would have lost his momentary spark of confidence and made his own way to the altar, which is where brazen boys who block girls in chapel pews belong.

I gently pulled my hands away and flopped on the papasan chair. "Jamie, you knew he was coming to talk to me? I can't believe you let him do that after I spent the whole altar time crying! Today's practicum with the kids in the projects was intense, and I really think God might be asking me to move here. I'm in no position to flirt with a boy! Look at me!"

She shrugged. Sure, it was easy for her to be ambivalent. It wasn't her hot messery on display.

"Jamie! I look terrible! My eyes are puffy, my face is blotchy, and I'm pretty sure there's snot on my shirt." I looked down to confirm. Yep, snot was drying as we spoke. Classy, Osheta. Straight-up classy.

Jamie looked me over again, and this time she grimaced. "Yeah, girl, you should probably do something about that before you see him tonight in the commons for the evening meeting. But whatever. You're still a beautiful girl. What did he say to you?"

I grabbed a makeup wipe from Jamie's shower caddy to dab the snot stain off my T-shirt. "Umm . . . well . . . that he thinks I'm beautiful," I said under my breath.

Jamie threw her pillow at me. "Wait! What?" she squealed.

"He said, 'I hope you don't mind me telling you this, but I think you're beautiful.' I mean, as far as Christian boy pickup lines go—"

Jamie squeezed in next to me in the too-small chair, grabbed my face, and grinned mischievously. "Girl. You've met a really cute boy who loves Jesus and missions! We've gotta get a plan together."

* * *

Jamie's plan worked. The white boy, who, I learned at our evening meeting, was named T. C., was indeed bold, and his boldness has completely rubbed off on me. Three years later, we said "I do" in Audubon Park in New Orleans, overlooking a lagoon, during Mardi Gras. The kids from the neighborhood we worked in sat in the front row, cheering louder than the adults. To help us save money, friends catered the reception, arranged flowers, and helped bake 150 heart-shaped red velvet cakes.

It was a simple and community-driven wedding—which is exactly what we wanted.

A few days later, T. C. and I were resting in a hammock on our honeymoon when, as newly married couples do, we started reminiscing about the beginning of our relationship. What I didn't know was that from the moment he saw me get out of the church van, he was unsure of how to approach me. He wasn't raised in church culture, so he didn't understand all the subtexts and rules.

"Why can't a man just tell a woman he's interested in that she's beautiful? Why do people seem to think that's some kind of sin?" he asked as we swung in the hammock, the waves gently crashing on the beach. I really wanted to reach for my fruity drink, but I was too comfortable nestling into the nook of his side.

"People just don't do that. Especially boys. We don't just go around telling people they are beautiful," I explained.

"Well, maybe there's a time for calling beauty *beauty*," T. C. started. "I really didn't expect you to run off like that! I honestly thought that you'd be so flattered, you'd stick around to talk!"

I chuckled. "Oh my goodness, are you kidding me? I was the furthest thing from beautiful that night. I mean, you saw me ugly crying up there. You know this by now: my face scrunches up like a gargoyle—it's terrifying. And then let's not talk about how my nose turns into a faucet anytime I feel big feelings. Either you were really out of your mind or you were trying too hard to get me. Because I was so not beautiful."

He tightened his arm around me and turned to look me dead in the eyes, "That's the thing, babers. You were beautiful. You are beautiful."

"Can I tell you something really funny?" I asked.

His eyes shone with anticipation of a secret. "Yeah?"

"I thought you were prophetically encouraging me," I said. "Like God told you to tell me that I was a beautiful woman. Jamie and I used to do that when we were both struggling with body issues. I hated being black, and she was fighting anorexia. Whenever we saw each other, we'd say, 'How are you today, Beautiful Woman?' or 'Beauty! Tell me something great that happened today.'"

He kissed my forehead. "See? There is a time for calling beauty when we see it. Everyone we meet is intrinsically beautiful. So I guess on one level, yeah . . . maybe God told me to tell you you're beautiful. We all reflect the *imago Dei*: the image of God."

This is how theologians sweet-talk their spouses, by the way. It's kinda like Nadia Bolz-Weber meets Nora Ephron. Equal parts deep thoughts about the kingdom of God, pet names, and gooey confessions. (Don't get me started on what budget meetings sound like in the Moore house.)

Remember how I said earlier we need to go back to the beginning to form our shalom practices? From the very beginning, beauty is at the center of shalom.

The light that breaks the darkness? Beauty.

The water giving way to make space for dry ground? Beauty.

The sun and the moon? Beauty.

The water teeming with life and the birds flying in formation? Beauty.

The livestock and the insects? Beauty.

Humankind: average, ordinary humans, both male and female, made in the very image of God? Beauty.

Let's not overlook this.

The Bible begins with a story of beauty breaking into the world to subdue the chaos. The writers of Genesis use the phrase *T'ov Me'od*, which roughly translates to "good," or "forcefully good." When ancient readers studied this text and they read the phrase *T'ov Me'od*, they probably imagined God, after finishing his creation of the world, stepping back and saying, "This is good. Everything in it is good, and the way they are relating to each other is good."

Including our bodies.

* * *

When we forget that God created this world as flourishing and beautiful, we are in danger of rejecting the shalom of God for our bodies. We forget that in the beginning, our bodies were called "very good."

Our world has standards about what constitutes a good, profitable, desirous body. Usually, it's a thin, white female body that's desirous.

A strong body turns a good profit in the field. A weak body—one that cannot fight back because it's been pumped with drugs—is a fantastic profit in the sex trade.

All this while it remains true that a white male body will get you a job, win you an election, and keep you safe if you happen to drive at night—or really, at any time of day.

What does that mean for the millions of people who do not meet these standards? It means we're susceptible to believing lies about beauty. Those lies make us feel beholden to a system that was never meant for us. So we starve ourselves, overfeed ourselves, cut ourselves, bleach ourselves, and stand in the mirror and whisper, "I hate myself."

This is why, for many years, I couldn't believe a white man actually wanted to marry me, a black woman. I didn't really believe he loved me for me. In this brown skin, I have often felt that he loves me in spite of it. I think back to that chapel meeting and I imagine it must have been my piety at the altar or my enthusiasm to love needy kids that he found beautiful. It couldn't have been this brown skin, right?

Never this skin.

* * *

When I was a little girl and could not fall asleep at bedtime, I would play a game in which I'd get one wish, any wish, granted. I'd lie in my bed, feeling invisible under the cloak of darkness, and whisper my wish under my breath: "I wish I were white."

Many little girls might say "I wish I were a princess" or "I wish I were a mermaid" or even "I wish I were a cowgirl" (I did live in Texas, y'all). I was fine with being all of those things—as long as I got to be a white princess, a white mermaid, or a white cowgirl.

With my dark brown skin and darker brown eyes, I was the "dark" daughter. I'm much darker than my mama, whose fair skin, long red hair, and sparking green eyes would have let her pass as white had it not been for her wide, flat, distinctly African American nose. I am much more like my daddy, with his cocoa complexion and ruddy cheeks.

Because Daddy made me feel normal—not beautiful, but normal—everything he said was gold. Perfection. Truth. So when he told me white people set the standard for beauty and success in America and that I would have to work twice as hard in school to have half of what they have, I took that to mean my dark skin was bad. A hindrance. A liability. I knew my brown would never be as good as most of my friends' peach, apricot, or white skin. This left me feeling like an outcast from both my white friends and the black kids at school. Because I was an overachiever, at times, I was bullied because I wasn't acting "black enough."

And so I would play my "I wish I were white" game and lose myself in this imaginary world. When I made my wish to my fairy godmother, she'd wave her wand with a sad smile, and magic dust would instantly fall over my curly hair, making it straight, shiny, blond, and smooth. Then my skin would lighten, bit by miraculous bit, until it was no longer bad brown but creamy, peachy perfection.

And oh, the adventures, the joys, the privileges, the acceptance from all the "cool" kids that White Osheta would enjoy.

White Osheta would still be me. I would still love Jo March, and the New Kids on the Block, and Steve Urkel—but I'd be better. Prettier. Acceptable.

Now, more than twenty years later and somewhat accepting of this brown skin I walk in, I still catch myself playing that old "I wish I were white" game. And oh, the adventures, the joys, the privileges, the acceptance I imagine I would have as Adult White Osheta. Sometimes, all these years later, I still wish I were white.

White Osheta would open the website of the latest, biggest, most exciting event for Christian women and automatically feel welcomed. She'd say, "This is a place for me to meet my Jesus tribe! Look, that speaker has my blonde hair and she has my blue eyes! Look, that girl has the same statement necklace I bought at Charming Charlie's. I'm totally going to register!"

Instead, Black Osheta notices when the only representation of her brown skin is at the bottom of the sidebar, or at the end of a row of Caucasian beauties—or buried way down on the "Our vision" page, to make sure everyone knows this group cares about diversity. Black Osheta's heart drops to her gut and she thinks, "If I go, will they welcome me there for me or for my skin? Does having a sprinkling of black faces in their crowd assuage their guilt over the lack of diversity? I just won't go—I don't want to be the only black person at this event. It's hard enough connecting with the white friends I have; why go and be someone's token?" This is a shame, since all Black Osheta wants is to know and be known.

White Osheta would go to a museum with her three kiddos and no one would ask if she is the nanny. In fact, not a single person would notice her and her three. In their white skin, they would see evidences that they belong in the halls of intelligence and education. They would know the history, so they could change the future. Their skin color would ensure the power and position they needed to do so.

As Black Osheta, I get asked—not infrequently—if I'm the nanny of these three children who bear my features but not my coloring. Why? I thought we moved past the assumption that black women are the "help." Then again . . . maybe not.

White Osheta could shop in upscale boutiques without a discreet employee tail. As she gushed at the soft cashmere sweaters, the shop owner would say to her, "Feel the quality; isn't it like butter?" White Osheta would rub her perfect white hand over the fabric while balancing a pumpkin spice latte in the other—no problem at all. She'd pull out her credit card and the store owner would not need to ask for ID. Her sweater would be wrapped with love, and she'd be sent on her way with a smile. "Please come back!" White Osheta would hear as she tossed her lovely hair.

As Black Osheta, I have to smile and strike up a conversation when I first walk into the store so that the staff know I'm trustworthy, well-spoken, and not prone to stealing. I guzzle down my latte just steps outside the store, because it's less embarrassing than being asked to throw it away in front of the other shoppers.

White Osheta would turn on a romantic film and instantly feel connected with the main characters. She could see herself in them and easily slip into their story. Escapism success!

As Black Osheta, I have to reimagine the heroine as African American. I spend half the movie wondering if that hot lead guy would ever date a black woman and the other half forcing myself to forget that if I were ever transported to Regency-era England, I'd be lucky to be offered a position as a servant.

When my sweet white friends call me up and want to hang out or "like" my Facebook status or want to talk *Scandal* with me—I don't want to question if they love me for me, or if they just want a black friend to ease the discomfort that years of oppression have woven into the fabric of black-white relationships. "Do they just want a black friend?" I wonder. Do I make it okay for them to say,

"I'm progressive/liberal/accepting," and "We're past race issues," and "I'm not a racist—I have a black friend"?

Affection is not necessarily reconciliation.

Black Osheta is always filtering her interactions with white women through the "token" lens.

"Do you love me, or do you want me to ease your discomfort?"

Honestly, I just want to be confident that they see me as I see them: beautiful, funny, ridiculously intelligent, God's best and bravest gift to me. This is a privilege that White Osheta blissfully enjoys: racial-lens-free living.

When the fantasy ends, it's time to go back to being Black Osheta. And to be honest, sometimes I don't want to.

* * *

I don't want to resent my skin; she has been faithful to me. She has endured frantic scrubbing to make the color go away and irrational hiding from the sun because "I don't want to get too dark."

My skin deserves to be loved. As much as the wide hips that bore my babies deserve grace. As much as my thick thighs deserve wonder for how they keep me upright, my creamy cocoa perfect brown skin deserves love. She protects my inmost parts—those secret places where God said he knew me before I was even born. She was there while big God breathed onto my little spirit. My skin stretched to contain the mystery of my newly formed *imago Dei*.

When God finished leaving his thumbprint on my heart, he noticed my skin. He saw how dark and rich she'd be, smiled, and said with pride and conviction, "You are forcefully good."

Forcefully good in this brown skin.

As I study shalom for my body, it's clear to me, that it wasn't enough for the writers of Genesis to set us free to believe that God made our bodies as good in order to quell insecurities and comparisons. No, according to Scripture our bodies are profoundly important in our partnership with God in bringing about shalom for the world. You see, because we are made in the image of God, we have dominion over the world. That word *dominion* is, as Lisa Sharon Harper said in an interview about her book *The Very Good Gospel*, "more like stewardship and protection." Harper went on to say, "All humanity is created with the call and capacity to exercise dominion." One of the ways we exercise our dominion in this world is to see the beauty in others and call it out. This is a practice of shalom we can all participate in. Like Adam in the garden, who was tasked with naming all the animals. He saw their unique beauty and gave them a name befitting that beauty.

A Shalom Sista is a woman who looks for the beauty in every person and calls it out because she is convinced that we are all image bearers of God. Because we believe every human is an image bearer of God, we are grieved when bodies of all kinds are mistreated.

In the life of Jesus, we see this same mission to honor the beauty of our bodies. We see it first in the incarnation: "The Word became flesh and made his dwelling among us. We have seen his glory, the glory of the one and only Son, who came from the Father, full of grace and truth" (John 1:14). We see it in his protection of marginalized bodies, as in the case with the woman caught in the act of adultery (see John 8:1-11). We see it in the Lord's Supper (see Luke 22:19).

Every Christmas we are reminded, through cute pageants and stirring carols, that God took on a body and lived among us. But let's not let the familiarity of this message rob it of its good news for us today. When Jesus took on a human body, he proclaimed its intrinsic beauty. When Jesus was a baby in the manger, yes, the shepherds worshiped, Mary sighed, and the cows lowed. But the deeper truth is that when Jesus was born, the divine, wrapped in a tender human body, was saying, once again, "It is good. It is very good." I love what theologian Dietrich Bonhoeffer said about the incarnation: "And in the Incarnation the whole human race recovers the dignity of the image of God."

Shalom Sistas, this is our calling too! When we realize that we are image-bearers, we are tasked with seeing the very same beauty in others and calling it out.

I know the whole "You're beautiful" trend can seem insensitive for some. A teenager once told me that when someone tells her, "You're beautiful," she immediately asks, "Why do you think that? You don't know me or know what I think is beautiful."

I get that skepticism. Beauty is not a thing that can be clearly defined and conformed to. Beauty, intrinsic beauty, is a kingdom value the Shalom Sista upholds every single time she says, "I will see the beauty and I will call it out."

Seeing the beauty empowers us for our divine responsibility to protect bodies—all bodies, but especially those that are marginalized because they do not conform to a false picture of beauty. This is one area in which I've learned I must become a peacemaker for myself before I make peace for others.

My friend Kacie practices this point of the Shalom Sista Manifesto nearly every day. She owns a shop called Persimmon Prints. When she came on my podcast as a resident Shalom Sista to talk about her journey with infertility, the very first thing I thanked her for was a product in her store: a mirror decal that says "You are beautiful." I have the decal on my bathroom mirror right now. It's captured in quite a few mirror selfies on my Instagram feed. The decal came as an add-on to an order, and when I saw it, I burst into tears. I didn't know how much I needed a complete stranger to speak this truth.

The very morning that the decal came in the mail, I realized my jeans were too small. Maybe I was too full from breakfast or they had shrunk in the wash? But deep down, I knew: I had gained weight. All day long, I told myself that I was lazy, careless, foolish, and "too big." I stayed in my pajamas until late in the afternoon— even going so far as picking the kids up from school in my bright pink paisley pj's. It was one of the few times I was grateful that our school has a drive-through carpool lane. When I got home, I found the wrap I had purchased, along with this little extra gift:

"You are beautiful" written in a gorgeous script. It immediately went on the mirror.

Kacie told me on the podcast that she first thought of the product to encourage teenage girls who were struggling with body image: to remind them that God sees their beauty and loves them for who they are. Soon after they were produced and placed on the market, women of all ages began sharing their stories with Kacie. Like me, they are so grateful for the reminder as they glance in the mirror each morning.

"I will see the beauty" it's our promise and purpose to proclaim the *imago dei* in every single person we meet— sometimes, including even ourselves.

So, my sweet Sista. I hope you don't mind me telling you this, but I think you're beautiful.

-8-

TREAT YO SELF? WE WILL REST

*One ancient practice to balance the future and present problem of
our culture is Sabbath.*
—**Kelly Gordon**

The one argument T. C. and I have with some regularity is about work. The argument takes various forms. Should I work outside the home? Should he take on another web design job in addition to his pastoral work? Is he spending too many hours in the office? How should we balance family with ministry?

I am the voice of work, work, work, work, work, work. I always want to add on a few more hours or look for one more side hustle. My position is that since I pay the bills, I have a better sense of what we need. I know what we need for extras like vacations, retirement, giving, and saving for the kids' tuition, so T. C. should listen and help me rearrange our life to earn more income. The outcome is worth the stress.

He disagrees (hence the arguing). He asks questions about the kids' schedules, their emotional health, my insecurities about the home's upkeep, and is it really worth it? My response? The kids' schedules are pretty open; they don't have many extracurriculars. I'm totally okay with giving them some extra screen time or playtime with friends after school while I work. I tell him I really don't care about whether the house is clean (which is a barefaced lie: I do care). But yeah, I think the extra income is worth the stress. I wouldn't be arguing with him if I didn't.

We go back and forth for at least twenty minutes and then he says, "Okay, babers. Tell me what Sabbath is going to look like for us if we take on this job."

Sabbath. He always wins with Sabbath.

He knows right now that with the schedule and responsibilities we have as a ministry family, we're doing the best we can to keep a rhythm of Sabbath. Adding anything else will throw off our fragile system.

When T. C. says "Sabbath," he is reminding me that the peace of Christ I'm looking for—shalom—won't come from the extra money, the new job connections, or the sense of accomplishment at work. When he says "Sabbath," he's reminding me that Jesus has told us that our rest is found in him. "Come to Me, all who are weary and heavy-laden, and I will give you rest," Jesus said. "Take My yoke upon you and learn from Me, for I am gentle and humble in heart, and you will find rest for your souls. For My yoke is easy and My burden is light" (Matthew 11:28-30 NASB).

And so T.C. rests his case, so to speak. At least for a while.

* * *

Sometimes when we talk about the world versus the kingdom of God, they look diametrically opposed: Violence versus self-sacrifice. Pride versus humility. Greed versus generosity. Slavery versus freedom.

When it comes to Sabbath and rest, however, we sometimes hear the same messages in the church that we read in *O* magazine. "Take time to care for yourself," "You deserve a break," "You've earned it," and "Treat yo self": these messages of self-care could come from the devotional booklet on my nightstand or the glossy fashion mag right underneath it. I once opened up Facebook to a whole feed of "Treat Yourself Day" images from my friends, who were celebrating the holiday inaugurated by the sitcom *Parks and Recreation*. My friends, many of them Christians, were having so much fun, and I was more than a little jealous of their pretty pedicures, new outfits, post-yoga glows, and clean houses because they had hired their cleaners for an extra day. #TreatYourself.

Now, Sista, I will be the first to look you in the eye and tell you that I have well-planned wish lists for fancy little treats and luxuries from all my favorite places. I am here for back rubs, chocolate croissants, and Netflix binges. I can self-care with the best of them. All day. Every day.

But maybe that's the problem. Maybe we have so saturated the market with a Sabbath-esque message of "self-care" that we don't know what Sabbath truly should be. I wonder if we've co-opted the world's messages and, in the process, diluted the true meaning of Sabbath. In a fascinating article in the *Atlantic* called "How 'Treat Yourself' Became a Capitalist Command," Ester Bloom notes this about the ways we treat ourselves: "American culture, with its typical anything-worth-doing-is-worth-overdoing attitude, has reduced self-care to buying stuff and, even more counterintuitively, to trying to become a more productive employee. In other words, active self-care was originally considered necessary to be a philosopher, typically for elite white men who had the luxury to sit and think. Now, America has democratized it by making it seemingly available to all—at least, for a price."

When counselors and other experts tell us to practice self-care, I know that they have good intentions, but I don't think self-care alone is a message that serves us well as Shalom Sistas. We're well versed on the need to rest, slow down, be present, and treat ourselves, but I think we need to take a new look at Sabbath. Maybe when Jesus calls us to find our rest in him, he's teaching us what rest and self-care look like in the kingdom of God. I have a feeling that it's more than yummy snacks and luxurious spa visits. What if Sabbath in the kingdom of God is wildly different from the headline to "Self-care, baby. You deserve it"?

* * *

Something I've grown to love about Jesus is that he was a terrific troublemaker. For good. For the kingdom. Always. There's a story in Matthew 12 where Jesus was already a source of annoyance for the religious leaders of the day. At this point, they were past the point of reasoning with him and had moved to full-on looking for ways to delegitimize him and his message that the kingdom of God had come near. You see, along with his fantastic troublemaking, Jesus was also bringing shalom to the broken in profound ways, emboldening them to ask hard questions and believe their worth. When that happens, the troublemaking for good spreads. A Shalom Sista is simply a troublemaker for good.

So our shalom lesson on rest begins on a Sabbath. The Pharisees were people who followed the letter of the law, especially the Ten Commandments, so they were vigilant about remembering the Sabbath and keeping it holy. When they saw Jesus' disciples eating grain they picked—breaking a Sabbath law of doing no work on the Sabbath—they called Jesus out on it. He answered them: "But if you had known what this means, 'I desire compassion, and not a sacrifice,' you would not have condemned the innocent. For the Son of Man is Lord of the Sabbath" (Matthew 12:7-8 NASB).

Then the Pharisees noticed a man with a shriveled hand in the synagogue. Seeing this precious image-bearer of God as a teaching tool and not a human being, they went on to ask Jesus, "Is it lawful to heal on the Sabbath?" (Matthew 12:10).

Instead of getting into a legalistic debate with the Pharisees (because religious people love to get lost in the weeds of knowledge), Jesus' response was to tap into their sense of compassion to an animal—a sheep that has fallen into a pit—to expose their misguided efforts.

> And He said to them, "What man is there among you who has a sheep, and if it falls into a pit on the Sabbath, will he not take hold of it and lift it out? How much more valuable then is a man than a sheep! So then, it is lawful to do good on the Sab-

bath." Then He said to the man, "Stretch out your hand!" He stretched it out, and it was restored to normal, like the other. But the Pharisees went out and conspired against Him, as to how they might destroy Him. (Matthew 12:11-14 NASB)

What I find so interesting is the Pharisees didn't argue with Jesus, because they knew he was right. The Pharisees prided themselves on reminding the Jews to be a people "set apart"; this is why the rules were so important to them. The laws defined their identity as the chosen people of God. On this point the Pharisees were themselves correct: when God established Israel, he created Sabbath as an alternative way of living in relation to the cultures surrounding them. From the beginning, God desired to have a people set apart, a people who uniquely reflected his goodness on earth. Israel was intended to be that model for us.

Sabbath, the rhythm of resting one day a week and one year every seven, was in direct contrast to the common message of productivity and greed. Once a week, the Israelites were to stop working—not just to rest but to proclaim that their identity, worth, value, and purpose were not tied to their output. "The first commandment is a declaration that the God of the exodus is unlike all the gods the slaves have known heretofore," Walter Brueggemann writes. "This God is not to be confused with or thought parallel to the insatiable gods of imperial productivity. This God is subsequently revealed as a God of mercy, steadfast love, and faithfulness who is committed to covenantal relationships of fidelity."

The Pharisees knew this, and they were fine with being a people set apart—as long as they could define the terms, which for them was adhering to a set of rules. But Jesus, knowing the spirit of the law is always better than the letter of the law, taught them Sabbath's intended purpose: once a week we slow down enough to fully experience both the compassion and mercy of God. This is how we are a set-apart people: not that we treat ourselves or religiously practice self-care, but that we make space for God's mercy and goodness to flow in and then through us. As we slow down, rest, and reject the pressures of the world, we help mercy and goodness flourish around us.

Jesus wasn't denying that it was the Sabbath. He wasn't denying that people should observe the Sabbath. He was simply calling
into question how they observed it. And he was giving us two
distinguishing elements of Sabbath in the kingdom of God: mercy
and goodness. This story in which Jesus assumes lordship over the
Sabbath tells us several things about Sabbath in the kingdom that
the Pharisees had overlooked.

One: Sabbath is good for reclaiming our identity as children
of God.

Two: Sabbath is often misunderstood as a day defined by the
activities we can't or shouldn't do. This paralyzes us from doing
the good deeds we can and should do.

Three: Sabbath is not for our self-congratulation but rather is
a practice of participating in God's reign of goodness and mercy.

* * *

When God created Sabbath as a rhythm for us, it wasn't simply to
curtail our addiction to work; it was to reinforce our identity as
image-bearers. Every single person is made in the image of God,
and Sabbath is an opportunity to proclaim that for ourselves and
to protect it in others. This is why even the poor stopped working
on the Sabbath.

"I rested, and so should you" is what we hear from God when
we look at the creation story. Genesis 2:2 tells us, "On the sev-
enth day he rested from all his work"; in concert with the fourth
commandment ("Remember the Sabbath day by keeping it holy,"
Exodus 20:8), the mandate is clear. This means, Sista, that our
practice of Sabbath should reflect the goodness of God our creator
and the mercy of God our king.

So when my husband questions me about our Sabbath practice,
he's not simply asking if we're going to be able to rest, practice
self-care, or treat ourselves. He's asking, how will taking this new
job or that freelance gig prevent us from loving, protecting, and

respecting the image of God in ourselves and in others? Adopting that way of thinking has transformed how I observe Sabbath and it's wildly different that what I learned in church as a child.

When I first heard in church that Christians were to observe the Sabbath, I was told it was a whole day—Sunday—on which we did not work. We went to church, had a good meal with our family, and reset our souls for the week.

This is one very valid way of observing the Sabbath. But what if you're hungry and you have to work two, sometimes three, jobs to keep food on the table? How do you "Sabbath" then? What about if you cannot go to church because you don't have a car, or because you feel isolated from Christian community, or because you're simply struggling to trust God? What does Sabbath look like then?

When a Shalom Sista says "I will rest," she proclaims mercy and goodness for every single person on this planet who is weary. She thinks about her rest, yes, but also about the rest of her sisters in need: the one who is feeding three children on a single income because her husband is on disability. When we say "We will rest," we plot goodness for the poor by thinking of ways to provide them rest. We offer to babysit, bring meals over so they don't have to cook, leave care packages with a favorite movie, fun family game, or a funny joke. We give weekend getaways to couples who need to reconnect. This counters the narrative that Sabbath keeping is only for the comfortable or wealthy—two-income families or those with more than they need. If we identify that others cannot themselves practice Sabbath because of constraints like poverty, then as shalom seekers, we look to facilitate opportunities for them to rest.

Thus "We will rest" is both a proclamation of countercultural living and a declaration of our calling. We are women of mercy and goodness.

* * *

I learned the power of creating Sabbath opportunity for those in need from my friend Michelle. As I shared in an earlier chapter, right after I had my daughter, Trinity, I went through therapy for postpartum depression. Thanks to the therapy, I was managing the depression. Nevertheless, I was drowning.

Under ten loads of laundry.

Sometimes this is still the case. If you can't find me—if I do not show up for our coffee dates and you don't see me at church, and if I've gone radio silent on Facebook and the kids are running around disheveled, dirty, and smelling of mildew—please come looking for me. When you walk into my home, follow the trail of dirty towels and crumpled jeans to the laundry room. There you will find me, passed out under a pile of laundry.

I've finally come to terms with the fact that I'll never get all the laundry clean. There will always be something in someone's basket. The people in my house are insistent on using a new towel every single time they shower, and just when I think I've gotten on top of it, my son will come home with an armful of gym clothes that need to be washed immediately.

I just wish someone had warned me when I was waxing poetic about becoming a stay-at-home mom. Before I had kids. If you are a young, eager mother, you might speak of staying home with your kids so you can spend more time with them and really pour truth into them. You might show off your children's director-approved Bible plan to get your kids "in the Word." You may have visions of making cookies, building Lego sets, and ending the day with a frolic in the park. No one tells you that all those things—the cookies, the lying on the ground to build with Legos, the frolicking in the park—make for dirty, dirty clothes. No one tells you, my dear Sista, about the loads and loads of laundry that three children ages four and under will create.

Let me be the bearer of truth: Laundry's gonna get you, Boo. Every single time. Also, Amazon delivers Tide in bulk. Happy shopping. And frolicking.

Right after I finished therapy and felt that I was managing my depression well, I was surprised by how overwhelmed I still felt by the sheer force of work that came with being a mom of littles. It was hard enough making sure these kids were alive by the end of the day. The laundry? Well, it kept getting pushed off and off and off, until finally I considered burning it all and starting afresh at Target. Part of the reason we stopped going to church as a family during that time was—you got it—the laundry. I was in survival mode. I whittled my kids' daily clothing use to one outfit: one pair of clean pants, one pair of underwear, one shirt, one towel. That was as large a load as I could manage each day; everything else was shoved in the closet.

My sweet husband knew that I was suffering from cabin fever, so one Sunday morning shortly after our daughter turned five months old, he said, "Let's just go to church this one Sunday; everyone is dying to see the baby!" He was right. After we arrived we didn't even have a chance to sit down before a line formed to hold baby Trinity. With every hug and outstretched hand to take the baby, I prayed that no one would notice that we had been wearing the same outfits we wore when many of them visited with casseroles and greeting cards just five months prior. No one seemed to notice. I think we still had that powdery fresh family-with-a-newborn novelty on us.

After the service, our church had a fellowship time, during which we could enjoy refreshments and catch up with one another. This was probably my favorite part of Sunday morning. (Well, my second favorite part. Sista: I have a confession. Until my youngest turned three, I only went to church for the childcare. I mean, I loved Pastor Dan, and his sermons were usually encouraging. But if we're being honest, the forty-five minutes without kids sitting on me, pulling on my cardigan, digging in their nose, and wiping their fingers on my lap—that gorgeous sliver of time was the only reason T. C. got me out of the house in my regulation laundry-crisis outfit. When a new mom comes to me all flustered and in need of a hug, I hug her and then tell her to find a church, but not necessarily for Jesus. Jesus is good, but get there for peace and quiet offered by the childcare. (I really don't think Jesus minds; he knows what's up.)

So I was sitting there in the fellowship time, balancing a plate of meatballs on my knees. My middle child, T. J., was grazing from my plate and the women were passing my baby around when Michelle came over and sat down next to me.

Let me tell you about Michelle. Michelle ran in a group of four brilliant women at our church. They had all attended Ivy League schools. Their children were older than mine, so they had that air of sanity that comes when you don't have to listen to the *Caillou* theme song on repeat. They all cared about justice in the city, but they still managed to take their kids on camping trips and wilderness hikes. They knew where all the best vacation Bible schools in the city were, and they all had season passes to every art and science museum within a fifty mile radius, including the zoos. They loved Jesus and quoted Scripture with a sincerity that actually made me want to memorize it too. They served faithfully in various roles at church nearly every Sunday, and they all took it upon themselves to care for the booming population of new moms in our congregation, myself included. When it was my turn, I wanted to be the same type of role model for young moms that they were to me.

So when Michelle sat down next to me, I knew she was on Mentor Mom business. She smiled at me and asked, "How are things going, Osheta?"

Somebody handed Trinity back to me, and I studied Michelle's face to see if her nose wrinkled at the slight mildew smell emanating from my baby's onesie. "I swear, Lord," I prayed silently. "Please let me not be embarrassed before I get through a plate of meatballs."

"We're doing great!" I told Michelle. "Thanks for asking." Michelle reached her arms out and asked to hold Trinity. One does not refuse a Mentor Mom who offers to take your baby, especially when the semi-warm meatballs your toddler is never going to finish are up for grabs. I placed Trinity in Michelle's arms and she patted Trinity's back. As she did so, she touched her nose to the baby's onesie and said, "The smell of babies is one of my favorite smells in the world; they're so sweet."

I was praising the Lord within my spirit that he had masked the stank of my baby. Or maybe babies just smell amazing to anyone who didn't birth them or feed them at three in the morning?

"Yeah, so sweet . . ." I trailed off while poking at a meatball. (Hold up! Did they simmer them in barbecue sauce? The Lord saw me and loved me.)

Michelle moved Trinity to her other shoulder as Trinity's eyes slowly closed. "You know, Osheta," Michelle started. "I've been thinking a lot about you. I realized the other day that Jim works close to you. So I was thinking: Maybe on his way to work, he could stop by your house and pick up a few loads of laundry. Then I could wash those clothes for you, and Jim could drop them off at your house on Friday. How does that sound?"

I sat there, stunned. First of all, how did she know I was overwhelmed with laundry? In the Pentecostal tradition, we have this phrase: "She read my mail." This is basically a churchy way of saying the Holy Spirit is Big Brother who has ratted you out to the Thought Police. That's how I felt: as if Michelle had read my mail and was forcing me to air all my dirty laundry—literally. I guess I'm still something of a Pentecostal refugee.

Michelle could sense my hesitancy, so she added, "Just for a few weeks! We could just see how it works for a few weeks; then that way, maybe you could get some rest. You can take a nap or catch up on a movie. You can maybe read a book. I know you like to write—maybe you can get some writing in?"

I didn't know how to receive Michelle's offer. When you take on any task, you want to feel like a competent person. The common notion is that if you can't handle all the facets of a job, then maybe you were all wrong for the job in the first place. I felt all wrong for motherhood—from the postpartum depression to the laundry. I knew I needed the help, but I didn't want to invite Michelle into my mess. My mess smelled, my mess was wrinkly, and my mess tripped me up every day. In truth, I needed help with my mess. The memory of weeping on the bathroom floor haunted me every time I passed a piling-up load. I desperately needed someone to take it off my plate, because I was feeling overwhelmed deep in my bones.

"Well . . . I suppose I could send the kids' stuff to you—"

"No!" Michelle interrupted. "Send whatever you need to have washed! I know T. C. is going back to work soon, and he's taking classes again. I'm sure he's going to need lots of clean clothes. So send with Jim whatever you need cleaned. I just want to help."

I nodded and finished up the meatballs. The next morning I passed off four loads of laundry to Michelle's husband, Jim.

The whole time that laundry was in her care, I second-guessed whether I should have let her help me. Yes, I needed help. We didn't have the resources, the time, or the energy to get all of it washed within a reasonable amount of time. There was just no way I could get all those loads done while still taking care of my family. Still, every day that week, I wondered, "Oh my gosh; what did I do?"

But here's the cool thing: My closets, which had once housed our dirty clothes, were finally empty. I could see the board games that were pushed to the back. I found a pile of library books that I thought I had lost. (They were way overdue, but when I called the library and explained my story, they extended the time.) With Michelle's help, I had a bagful of books and a few hours of free time in the week. Since I wasn't trying to fit in a load here or there, I could sit down with one of those books while the kiddos napped. In releasing my laundry to Michelle, I also cast off the weight of "Failure," of "Do more," and of "Git 'er done." I walked through my home, light and hopeful once again, breathing a sigh of relief that I hadn't known my lungs had needed for the past five months.

That Friday morning, Jim stopped at my door, gave me the load of laundry and a little note from Michelle that said: "If you need it again next week, just let me know."

Michelle ended up washing my laundry for several months. To this day, whenever I mention it to her, she shrugs it off as just something that Christians do.

Yes, that's right. Helping others find rest is just something Shalom Sistas, ambassadors of Christ's mercy and goodness, do.

-9-

A STRANGE SONG: WE WILL CHOOSE SUBVERSIVE JOY

I believe in kindness. Also in mischief. Also in singing, especially when singing is not necessarily prescribed.
—**Mary Oliver**

The winter of 2015 was the harshest winter in Boston my family ever experienced. In addition to the usual ten feet of snow, freezing rain, and icy sidewalks, we were without a car. For six months. It's a long story, one involving an oil change gone wrong at a shop whose insurance refused to pay to replace the engine. When I told my mom in Texas what was going on, she worried out loud, "But, Osheta! How are you guys going to get around?" The idea of our family relying on public transportation in that cold weather—well, she just couldn't handle it.

Frankly, given all the frustrating elements of the oil-change-gone-wrong experience, relying on Boston public transit called the "T" was actually an adventure I welcomed. The closest train station to our home was the Harvard station, and it was an easy fifteen-minute ride on the 73 bus. From there we would jump on the Red Line and could get to just about anywhere in Boston. Even though I got lost a few times, once I figured out my best routes, I could just sit back with a good book or new podcast. My friend Boyd says if there's any city to be in without a car, it's Boston. It's true. The T is the best. It is efficient and clean, there are always amazing street performers at the major stations, and of course, y'all, there are a Dunkin' Donuts and funky coffee shops at nearly every stop. Relying on the T forced me to slow down, plan, and feel a certain solidarity with the commuters. Some of my favorite times on the T were during rush hour, when I got to see a beautiful mixture of people.

About six weeks into our car crisis, we got a letter saying our insurance company was going to refuse payment for the tow truck we needed to hire to get our car to another shop after the first shop's mistake. After I read the news, I needed to get out of the house to clear my head. That was another $300 we didn't have.

So I stood at the bus stop, looking at my phone for something cheap to do either in Harvard Square or near the next stop on the line, Porter Square. Paper Source was offering a discount for their card-making class if you checked in on Yelp, so I decided to treat myself. Just so you know, I have a box filled with pretty greeting cards for nearly every occasion—it's my little obsession. I get this from my godmother, Missy. She remembers everyone's birthday and celebrates it with the perfect card. It's a spiritual gift, truly. I can't tell you the number of times I opened a card from her and the message was exactly what I needed to read. Naturally, I picked up this gift from her. I buy cards after holidays at a discount so that they're ready for next year, and I have a whole set of reminders on my phone just so that I can remember people's special days. I raid the Papyrus sale every single year. Listen. If there is anything you get from this book, I hope you remember this: it is time to reclaim the lost art of sending handwritten notes and greeting cards. Sistas, there's something magical about getting a card with a hand-stamped message or an embossed ribbon on the front.

When I got to the class, there were tables filled with stock paper in vibrant pastels, stamps, glitter, and ribbons. I'm not a particularly crafty girl, but you give me glitter and I'll give it the old college try. Glitter gives me life.

On my way home from card class, I stopped at my favorite coffee shop, Bourbon, and picked up a white chocolate mocha. Then I jumped on the bus, fingers shiny from the life-giving glitter and purse brimming with homemade greeting cards.

I settled into my seat for the fifteen-minute ride home on a relatively empty bus. I was looking forward to the quiet and calm my soul needed before I had to face a budget conversation with T. C. Unfortunately, that was not in the cards for me. Across from me sat a young African American man spinning a dusty Spalding basketball on his fingertip. He wore a do-rag on his head, which he swung to the beat of the music in his earbuds.

Now, I think I must come from crotchety folk, because whenever I can hear people's music through their earbuds, something rises in me and I want to slap someone. This is how I started to feel about Spalding Spinner. His music was so loud, and he was tapping out the beat with his foot with such abandon. He was fully embodying the joy of the moment, when suddenly he burst into rap. Out loud. On the 73 bus.

Let me explain to you the 73 bus line. The 73 goes from Harvard Square to Belmont, which is one of the most conservative, most affluent neighborhoods bordering Cambridge. Spalding Spinner and I were the only black people on the bus. The rest of the passengers were three white men who looked like they might be professors coming home from teaching classes at Harvard; a young Asian woman in scrubs—possibly a medical student; an older couple reading the newspaper; and the bus driver, a gregarious man who would fit every single one of your Bostonian stereotypes.

Spalding Spinner started rapping louder and louder. The more confidently he rapped along with the music in his head, the more uncomfortable I felt for him. I watched him, the only black man on the bus, with his Air Jordans, his baggy coat, his gloveless hands ashy from the biting cold. I watched him spinning his basketball, tapping his foot, and rapping out lyrics hard and fast, primal and powerful. He was oblivious to the sharp sideways glances of the others on the bus, including me. "Why? Why are you doing that?" I wanted to ask him, my aggravated mama stare keen on the back of his head. "Stop it!" I wanted to tell him. "Don't you care that everybody is staring at you? Don't you know that you represent all brown bodies, and that you're making a scene?"

I didn't know it then, but Spalding Spinner was a powerful example of subversive joy. While the rest of us watched and listened in annoyed disbelief, he just kept stringing his rhyming words together. He was present to the goodness right around him, not letting the fact that he was brown or male or feared keep him from his joy.

He just kept spinning his Spalding. He kept abandoning himself to his joyful art, so beautiful and so baffling.

The whole fifteen minutes to my home, he never stopped swinging his head.

* * *

When I read about another bombing.

When I hear the word *yuge*.

When I receive another disappointing update from my friends who are fighting human trafficking in India.

When I walk by an older homeless man in a wheelchair who relies on an oxygen mask to breathe.

When another hurricane destroys another city.

When I hear a child cry.

When I see flashing lights in my rearview mirror.

For years now, these events and others have made me feel as tender as an exposed nerve. Sometimes when I'm reminded of some brokenness in the news, it's as if some essential organ in me throbs in red-hot pain. The constant buzzing, beeping, chiming, and scrolling of news has made us more susceptible to heartbreak around the world. Before we have a chance to process one news story, another of equal devastation pops up on our phones.

We are seeing history repeat in unsettling ways—violence, division, greed, and exhaustion of our earth's resources, to name a few. Joy amid all of this seems irresponsible—a Pollyanna optimism that borders on insensitivity. What is there to celebrate or enjoy when there are protests and bombings? Historian Walter Benjamin wrote that history is "one single catastrophic event which keeps piling wreckage upon wreckage," and I wonder whether he was onto something. When the wreckage fills my social media feeds, I turn to T. C. and exclaim, "What is going on in the world?"

When this happens, I feel myself pulling away from people. I get in my footie pajamas and hole up in my bedroom with Netflix. I journal improbable plans to save my family—moving, prepping, praying, hiding. It never seems enough. I feel nauseated, but I can never throw up. I cancel meet-ups with friends because I'm scared of getting sick, or being the buzzkill, or ugly crying. I don't think I'm depressed; I just think I'm done. Done with the world altogether. If I could justify changing my view of the end times so that Jesus will whisk us away to never suffer again, while all the wicked people are left to clean up the mess they mad, well, I would. Unfortunately, my picture of God doesn't allow for that.

I know we are made whole to be a part of God's plan to make the world whole. But where does our peace come from when it feels as though our lives are one big trigger warning? The truth is, sometimes I'm an ambassador of wholeness with a perpetually broken heart.

A broken heart for the world's brokenness isn't necessarily a bad thing. When my children hurt, the compassion I have for them is good, even though it feels terrible in the moment. Shalom Sistas are women who are deeply in touch with our compassion for everyone, which makes us particularly vulnerable to despair and hopelessness.

But there's one weapon I've begun trying to deploy when I feel overwhelmed: joy. Miroslav Volf gives us a compelling argument for including joy in our formation as shalom seekers.

> The Bible invites individuals and communities to practice and participate in God's true joy. After telling the disciples that they

should keep his commandments and remain in his love, Jesus explains, "I have said these things to you so that my joy will be in you and your joy will be complete." Joy is the crown of the good life, integrating all positive emotions as well as including and expressing in its own way the responsibility to lead our lives well and to construe both the world and the good rightly. Yet joy is not usually the first word that comes to people's minds when asked about Christianity or the church. What if it was?

What if, indeed. Our apprehension about choosing joy might be because we've been given a thin definition of joy as something like "a feeling of great pleasure and happiness," with flimsy examples to follow. The joy of the kingdom of God is more durable, subtle, and lasting than our common definitions of joy.

One morning I was stuck in bed. I had just watched a newscast about violence in the Middle East, and I couldn't move. My body felt heavy. I kept seeing the children's faces bloodied, the demolished buildings, the body count rising.

Lying there, I wanted to reject my calling as a Shalom Sista to care and protect the image of God in people. I wanted someone to come and worry about caring and protecting me. I was, in truth, sad. So very sad.

My daughter came into the room and nuzzled next to me, completely aware of the despair I was battling, and said, "Mama . . . wanna hear a really funny joke?"

Now a word about comedy in the Moore house. If you want to be our friend; if you want to make our Christmas card list and be the first ones we run to during fellowship time; if you want us to spend time on your porch late into the night, then you must make at least one of us laugh. Not all of us. Just one of us.

There are five of us Moores, and we have five distinct comedic personalities. I'm quirky and a little irreverent. T. C. is dry and slightly derisive. Tyson, the fifteen-year-old, is just like his dad, but add a few fart jokes in there and you've got him rolling on the floor with laughter. T. J. is our twelve-year-old, and he's quiet, so observational humor is his strength. When he makes a joke, it's gonna land. That boy has the best comedic timing. Trinity is eleven, and she has been competing with guys all her life, so you never know what might come out of her mouth. She's my little Melissa McCarthy. It could be a knock-knock, or it could be a joke about toe jam. You just never know with the only girl. But every joke will be punctuated with a sassy head wobble. It's her trademark and inheritance.

Which is why I hesitated. "Um . . . sure you can tell me a joke," I said a bit wearily, pulling myself up a little.

"What do you call cheese that doesn't belong to you?" she said, suppressing her giggles.

"I don't know, Trin. What do you call cheese that doesn't belong to you?"

She sat up, puffed out her chest, and announced in her most indignant voice, "Nach-o cheese."

Head wobbling, just like her mama taught her.

✳ ✳ ✳

I will not be ashamed of this: I am so here for '80s kids' movies. One of my favorite icebreakers is "What are your top five 1980s kids' movies?" If your list does not include *The Neverending Story*, then I'm not sure we can be friends. Shalom Sistas, sure, but friends, questionable.

The Neverending Story is a live-action fantasy movie about a quiet boy named Bastian with a wild imagination, a love of reading, and a grief over the loss of his mother. He is chased by bullies right into a bookstore one morning before school, and the owner soon realizes he's a special boy with a mature appetite for books. So he leaves a very rare, very powerful book out on the counter while he takes a phone call. Bastian steals the book, runs to school, hides from the bullies, and gets lost in the story about a dying land, Fantasia. Fantasia is slowly being overtaken by a force called the Nothing. The Nothing looks like storm clouds, but as it passes over the beautiful, vibrant land of Fantasia, it disappears. Leaves nothing behind. No crater. No rubble. Nothing.

The high council of the land calls for a warrior to fight the Nothing, and a prairie boy name Atreyu answers their call. Bastian immediately identifies with Atreyu's journey. But there is one element in particular that Bastian connects with profoundly: the Swamps of Sadness.

The Swamps of Sadness are where all the despair of Fantasia rests. Fantasia itself is a glorious place, but the swamps are where the brokenness lives. They are also the home of Morla the Ancient One, who knows how to stop the Nothing. To become the warrior he needs to be in order to truly champion Fantasia, Atreyu must walk through the swamps and not let the sadness overtake him. If he does, he'll sink and die. On the journey with him is his gorgeous horse and best friend, Artax. Midway through the swamps, Artax begins to sink—slowly, inch by inch, until his noble white mane is covered in mud. Even though Atreyu begs him to fight the sadness, Artax cannot. And so, with a heart-wrenching organ theme behind Atreyu's screams, the screen cuts to black. We as viewers don't have to be told. Artax dies because he gives in to the sadness.

That. Movie. Messed. Me. Up.

There's something we can learn from Atreyu and Artax, though. Sadness is not something we can avoid. To be the warriors our brokenhearted world needs, we must allow ourselves to feel sadness, deeply. But we must not sink too deeply into that sadness. We need to practice subversive joy: a joy that resists despair.

My favorite description of joy comes from theologian Willie James Jennings. "Joy is an act of resistance against despair. . . . [Joy] resists despair and all the ways that despair wants to drive us toward death," Jennings said in an interview. "Death in this regard is not simply the end of life, but it's death and all its signatures—death, violence, war, debt, all the ways in which life can be strangled."

Joy as an act of resistance to death and all its signatures: this definition fits into our framework as women of the kingdom of God who seek to live counterculturally. When we practice joy in desperate times, we sing the battle hymn of the kingdom of God in a strange land, as does the psalmist in Psalm 137.

By the rivers of Babylon we sat and wept
  when we remembered Zion.
There on the poplars
  we hung our harps,
for there our captors asked us for songs,
    our tormentors demanded songs of joy;
    they said, "Sing us one of the songs of Zion!"
How can we sing the songs of the Lord
  while in a foreign land? (Psalm 137:1-4)

Instead of singing along to our song, the world will always tell us, "You should be ashamed! Look at all the suffering! How can you find joy?" Even so, a Shalom Sista chooses joy as an act of resistance against despair. She continues to sing her song of wholeness and hope. We persist in telling a counterstory: that in the kingdom of God we never lose sight of joy. For joy, as C. S. Lewis says, is "the serious business of heaven."

I once heard a story about Brownies in a Chinese concentration camp who practiced subversive joy. During World War II, Japan occupied China, built concentration camps, and then gathered up American, British, and other European civilians living in China. For four years, they treated the prisoners, many of whom were young children, terribly.

In one camp called Weihsien, teachers who were prisoners had brought supplies along with them to the camp, including two curious items: girls' club uniforms and musical instruments. I mean, I have a little experience packing quickly for disaster, and I could see bringing books and clothes, but musical instruments? Insensible, no?

The teachers also packed Girl Guide uniforms. Here in the United States, an equivalent would be Girl Scouts. I know a thing or two about the Scouts. I taught dance for two summers at a Girl Scouts camp, and in our orientation we were taught, "If you can sing it, you should." And sing we did. As we walked from the cafeteria to the beach. When we woke our charges up. When we greeted them in the morning. When we comforted the homesick. When we saw them off at the end of camp. There was so much singing. I loved every moment of it.

The Girl Guides of Weihsien knew the power of song too. Mary Previte, a survivor of Camp Weihsien, was just a little girl when she became a Girl Guide in the concentration camp. In an interview at the age of eighty-two, after recounting the horrors of bayonet drills, electrified wires, and guard dogs, she said that singing her song of joy in a strange land is what saved her. "We were constantly putting things into music," she said.

> Often, there was a little bit of a twist of fun to it. . . . One of the things that we sang when the Japanese were marching us into concentration camp was the first verse of Psalm 46: "God is our refuge, our refuge and our strength," and on it goes, "in trouble we will not be afraid." All of these words just sung into our hearts. That sticks. It's like you've got a groove sticking in the gramophone record. I am safe, I am safe, I am safe. That was just profound.

I cannot think of a place that poses more pain triggers and opportunities to slip into despair than a concentration camp. If these young girls could harness the power of joy—if they could let that joy create a groove in their souls that they were safe—then I know I can too. I can practice subversive joy in the face of all those pain triggers.

When I see a new baby at church.

When I taste fresh sweet potato fries.

When I wrap up in a blanket.

When my husband brings me flowers.

When the sun rises between the foothills.

When I get an actual letter in the mail.

When my favorite top is clean.

When anything by Carrie Underwood comes on the radio.

When my daughter tells a joke.

All these and more are my joy triggers. These small acts help me practice subversive joy. I will not let the despair get to me. I will continue to sing my song in a strange land.

I want to be a woman who recognizes the small pleasures God provides right here, right now. I want to have the courage to hold both pain and joy in tension with each other. Jesuit priest James Martin writes that joy "does not ignore pain in the world, in another's life, or in one's own life. . . . Rather, it goes deeper, seeing confidence in God—and for Christians, in Jesus Christ—as the reason for joy and a constant source of joy."

So take heart, Sista. We are not overcome. We do not have to sink into sadness. We can sing and look for joy triggers. We can sit up, pull ourselves out of bed, and laugh at our daughters' ridiculous jokes. We can choose subversive joy.

PART IV

Shalom in Our Relationships

-10-

CARPOOL TRIBUTE: WE WILL TELL BETTER STORIES

We must learn to regard people less in light of what they do or omit to do, and more in the light of what they suffer.
—Dietrich Bonhoeffer

The angry woman in the baby-poop green Jeep has just flipped me off. We are both in the carpool lane at school—or as I like to call it, the Vehicular Hunger Games. Everyone is some degree of angry, hungry, hot, tired, or annoyed that we have to take our children back (seriously, can't they just stay for one more hour?). No one would admit it, but we all want to roll our windows down and yell at the crossing guard—really, what is he doing, stopping traffic for no reason? Even the grandmother in the 2004 Mercedes Benz—even she's eager to tell off the man while Barry Manilow blasts from her radio.

Invariably, in the carpool lane someone will get flipped off, cussed out, or honked at. Even worse, someone will be approached while waiting for their babies.

Today, it is my turn to be the tribute.

Jeep Driver pulls over and runs up to my car while I'm at the stop sign, ready to pull out of the parking lot. True story. With my kids in the car and her kids watching from hers, she assaults me with choice cuss words and a promise to turn my license plate in to the administration.

For context, Sistas, I have just broken an unspoken carpool lane law. I accidentally pulled in front of her to where my kids were standing on the curb. I was supposed to pull up *behind* her, wait for her kids to load up, and then pull forward to retrieve mine. Carpool politics, man—they'll get you every time. I didn't wait my turn, and so now it's going down in the carpool lane.

Y'all remember how I'm not your typical peacemaker? Right. So now she's yelling at me just inches from my face, and I'm so close to showing her that this tribute don't play . . . when I remember two things.

1. My babies are watching.

2. I am a Shalom Sista.

"What do you have to say for yourself?" justified-in-her-frustration Jeep Driver asks.

I will tell a better story, I will tell a better story, I will tell a better story, I think over and over again, until clarity comes.

"Um, I'm sorry and I didn't realize I was making a mistake until too late. Thanks for letting me know! Have an awesome day, okay?" I say each statement with a little trepidation in my voice and as little snark as possible. She could escalate this. If she does, I'm not sure I can hold it together—I'll either cry or cuss.

The cars behind us begin to honk, so Jeep Driver harrumphs and goes back to her car. My kids release the breaths they've been holding.

"Oh, Mama . . . she was *so* mad at you!" my daughter says, giggling. Laughter is her defense mechanism. Plus, it was actually funny how angry Jeep Driver was.

"Yeah, she was pretty ticked," I say, putting the car in gear and turning off the radio that had been playing quietly in the background. "But she probably had a long day, and it's really hot. I bet she just wanted to get her kids from school and get home, and me pulling in front of her slowed her down."

I'm beginning to tell a better story about Jeep Driver. This time she's not my opposing tribute but an overwhelmed mom of four sitting in the oppressive heat of Southern California.

"Teej," I call to my middle child, T. J., because we're about to play his favorite game. "Tell me something that happened to that woman today before pickup that made her so angry."

He begins to spin a tale of an annoying boss who ruined her perfectly organized desk when he sat down on the edge of it. He says she had a blown tire on her way home, and a soggy tuna fish sandwich for lunch. This is our family shalom practice when someone annoys us: we give them a compassionate backstory to help us forgive them. We hope that it reinforces the better stories we tell about their misbehavior.

"Trin, what do you think tomorrow is going to be like for the woman in the Jeep? What should I do in the carpool lane?" I ask.

"Well," she begins, with authority in her voice. "You should wait your turn. Don't pull in again! But when you see her, you should smile at her. That way she'll know you're not mad." This, planning to be kind, is our final act of forgiveness toward Jeep Driver.

"Good call, girl," I say, as we pull into our parking spot outside our apartment.

I've often wondered, at what point does another person become my enemy? When she flips me off? When she approaches my car? When she embarrasses me in front of my babies?

According to Jesus, people are never our enemies. A Shalom Sista knows this, and so when people hurt her, she will tell better stories.

* * *

Telling better stories is our commitment to Jesus' teaching in Matthew 5.

You have heard that it was said, "Love your neighbor and hate your enemy." But I tell you, love your enemies and pray for those who persecute you, that you may be children of your Father in heaven. He causes his sun to rise on the evil and the good, and sends rain on the righteous and the unrighteous. If you love those who love you, what reward will you get? Are not even the tax collectors doing that? And if you greet only your own people, what are you doing more than others? Do not even pagans do that? Be perfect, therefore, as your heavenly Father is perfect. (Matthew 5:43-48)

These instructions from Jesus always seemed so problematic for me, but it's hard to ignore that we follow an enemy-loving God. From the cross, Jesus loved his "enemies" when he cried out, "Father, forgive them." He told a better story when he said, "For they know not what they do!" It's true: they didn't know what they were doing, and Jesus chose to see that. He chose to see where they were innocent when he could have focused on the horrible things they did. That is enemy love: looking past a person's anger, hatred, violence, and fear that are directed toward you to offer forgiveness and the benefit of the doubt.

When a Shalom Sista says "I will tell better stories," she is asking the Holy Spirit to empower her with the same forgiveness that Jesus displayed on the cross. She is asking for eyes to see the fear behind the violence, the sadness behind the anger, the person behind the behavior.

There's a quotation going around right now that truly bothers me. It's common-sense advice on how you should handle people's bad behavior: "When a person shows you who they are, believe them."

Can I suggest a slight but shalom-inspired change: when a person shows you who they are, believe that they didn't get there on their own and tell a better story about them.

Okay, listen to me: I am so here for boundaries and wisdom and appropriate circles of intimacy. Enemy love should never be used as a weapon to beat us into submission if we're in toxic relationships. Enemy love is our peacemaking mechanism when we encounter hurting people: it reminds us of their humanity, their immeasurable worth to God, and it protects our hearts from hate.

When I suggest that peacemakers practice enemy love, I often hear this response: "Well, if you love your enemies and reflect the cross-shaped love of Christ for your enemies, aren't you inviting mistreatment or, at the very least, condoning their behavior?"

Well, no and yes.

No, because we are to be wise as serpents, yet gentle as doves. God gave us a brain and instincts for a reason. If someone is consistently hurtful to you, then as an image-bearer of God charged with protecting the image of God in both yourself and the person hurting you, you have the right to say, "I love you enough to not let you continue hurting me. We need some space; please seek some help." You can do this and still love the person. You can do this and still tell yourself a better story about that person. Self-respect and enemy love are not mutually exclusive.

Yes, because hurt people hurt people. When we decide to courageously love people who have been broken by this world, they will inadvertently hurt us. They hurt Jesus, and they will hurt us. Jesus even promised this in John 15:20: "Remember the word that I said to you, 'A slave is not greater than his master.' If they persecuted Me, they will also persecute you; if they kept My word, they will keep yours also" (NASB).

Every time we choose to love those who hurt us, we make ourselves vulnerable. Yet in all my years of seeking shalom in my relationships, I've learned that love is the only force more powerful than anger or revenge. Love empowers us to forgive, and forgiveness is the scaffolding on which our better stories are built.

We tell better stories because we have been invited into God's magnificent story of redemption. There's always room to pen one more character arc, one more page of dialogue though hard conversations, one more hero's journey, one more victory. We have been made whole to make the world whole. We start with telling better stories about the people who hurt us.

* * *

It took me a week to get up the nerve to read the reports of the Steubenville rape case. You may remember this story. In the small town of Steubenville, Ohio, in 2012, a party got out of hand, ending with two star football players being arrested for raping a girl. The girl had been repeatedly sexually assaulted while peers at the party broadcast the acts on social media.

I didn't want to look closely at the case of the Steubenville teenage rape case, because I knew I would be prone to anger and disgust. As a mother of boys, I wondered if I was doing enough to teach them to respect women. As a woman, I was disappointed that patriarchy and rape culture still thrived. As a survivor of sexual assault, I ached to defend and protect the girl.

Not ready to face the barrage of emotions, I simply avoided the headlines and newscasts. Until.

Until the day I saw a photograph of one of the teenagers convicted of the rape, Ma'lik Richmond. Upon receiving his verdict, he openly wept on his lawyer's shoulder. The caption of the photograph reported Ma'lik's cry: "No one is going to want me now."

And something broke in me.

No one is going to want me now. I had once uttered those very same words. I had said them in the aftermath of my assault.

The details of our stories were wildly different, of course. I was the victim of sexual assault; they were the perpetrators. But because their pain made them more human to me, I could see the story from a different angle. I once had felt unwanted and unloved. So did they. I had wondered what was going to happen to my life after tragedy. So did they. I had needed the comfort of a shoulder. So did Ma'lik.

With the help of Carolyn the Confident and the study of my belovedness, I now tell myself a better story than the one of self-hatred. Whenever I feel the anguish of thinking no one wants me, I tell myself a better story: that I am beloved. Stopping and truly looking at the boys moved me to tell a better story about their belovedness. Now that I was open to crafting a better story for the

Steubenville teens, I wondered if there was someone in Ma'lik's and Trent's lives who could tell them that story. Who would tell them, "Someone wants you"?

Left with only my raw, vulnerable heart and a picture of a Savior who specializes in restoring the broken, I began to look around to see how the church was responding to these boys. Who was eager to tell the boys a better story?

My heart broke anew at what I found. All the Christian blog posts and articles on the rape case that I could find were about teaching our boys to be better, about rejecting the slut-shaming practices of rape culture, or about allowing ourselves to acknowledge our own sexual trauma. These were good pieces, for sure. Still, I could find no one who was telling a better story, a hopeful one. No one was speaking forgiveness and love over these boys.

I decided to write a blog post for the Steubenville rapists.

*   *   *

This post about the Steubenville rape case will be different because I'm not angry. I'm not horrified. I'm not justified, anxious, or indignant. Others are, but I'm not.

I'm broken.

I'm heartbroken for these boys. Regardless of what they've done or what a court has ruled, Someone does want Ma'lik Richmond and Trent Mays—and they don't know it.

Someone wants them, but it seems the body of Christ is silent on this truth. Maybe in an effort to side with justice, we're intentionally rejecting grace, but stripped down and bare before God about my assault and my own sinfulness, I'm too humbled to reject grace. You see, but for the grace of God, there go I. But for the grace of God, there go my boys.

But, by the grace of God, God wanted me.

In light of this mercy, I'm moved to stop and write this post that says "Someone wants these boys."

Our beautiful Someone—who sought table fellowship with the chief tax collector and washed the feet of his betrayer—wants Ma'lik Richmond and Trent Mays. Our humble Someone, who died while his closest friends scattered, wants these boys. Our scandalous Someone, whose greatest offense was the company he kept (the lowlifes, the violent, the unclean, and the outcast), wants to keep company with the Steubenville rapists.

Examine any story of Jesus and this reality glares at us: kingdom people are sinners whom Someone wanted.

What should we do, kingdom people? In light of this truth, what should I do? When I'm faced with the image of God doing the work of Satan, how should I respond?

With love, goodness, and humility.

As much as it's against my nature as a mama, a woman, and a survivor, I believe the kingdom response to these boys, whose choices have made them my enemy, is to love them and to be willing to take my lead from Jesus: our Someone, who washed the feet of his betrayer and prayed for his torturers' forgiveness while nailed to a cross.

Not to stroke my self-righteous ego but to proclaim "Someone wants you!" in response to Ma'lik's desperate cry.

To say that loving my enemy is wicked hard would be an understatement.

When I signed on with Jesus to embrace peace for forty days, I thought, "Cool, cool, Lord. I'm all types of stressed out, and you're going to wave your hand, throw a 'Peace, be still' in there, and peace is going to flow like a river! You know, I'm all about that peace that surpasses all understanding. So let's do this. Peace me out, yo!"

But no. Peace is looking more and more like Jesus' teaching in Luke 6:32-36, which says that to truly be at peace, I need to be a fast forgiver and a sure lover of my enemies.

If you love those who love you, what credit is that to you? Even sinners love those who love them. And if you do good to those who are good to you, what credit is that to you? Even sinners do that. And if you lend to those from whom you expect repayment, what credit is that to you? Even sinners lend to sinners, expecting to be repaid in full. But love your enemies, do good to them, and lend to them without expecting to get anything back. Then your reward will be great, and you will be children of the Most High, because he is kind to the ungrateful and wicked. Be merciful, just as your Father is merciful.

Couple this with these descriptions of God's mercy, and I'm undone: "The Lord our God is merciful and forgiving, even though we have rebelled against him" (Daniel 9:9). "But you, O Lord, are a God of compassion and mercy, slow to get angry and filled with unfailing love and faithfulness" (Psalm 86:15 NLT).

I'm completely wrecked because I don't have forgiveness swagger like that! I'm not slow to anger and quick to love. I enjoy clear lines of us versus them. Sometimes I like being a Christian because I get to be the good guy who fights for righteousness while my enemies stand wicked and unjust.

But what I'm learning is that my enemy isn't just the person who has offended me, or the terrorist who haunts my nightmares, or the sinner on the other side of the line. My enemy is the person whose actions, attitudes, and words are just beyond my empathy.

My enemy looks like Trent Mays, the white boy who had it all and threw it away. My enemy looks like Ma'lik Richmond, the black kid in a hoodie who resembles my abuser and every villain in our society's erroneous cautionary tale of "hoodlums and hooligans."

They are my enemies—the perfect combination of past hurts and future fears—the ones just beyond my empathy.

I didn't get that until I paid closer attention to the Steubenville case. I didn't get that until I chose to see the people behind the offense.

Now these verses directly challenge my assumptions and ask me to love them, to be more gracious than common courtesy, and to be merciful as my Father is merciful.

Jesus asks me to do it, and so I will—not just for my peace and not just for his glory, but for their redemption. I will love these boys even though they did something wholly unlovable. Our faithful, unconditional love for our enemies has the power to spread the gospel that:

Jesus wants them.

Jesus died for them.

Jesus loves them.

We are in danger of dishonoring Jesus by picking up the sword of angry, accusatory words against people when he's prepared to sacrificially love and accept them.

* * *

As I wrote that post, I kept thinking, "These boys have a chance to live into a better story. It's our job to tell them."

When a Shalom Sista says she will tell better stories, she is committing to look at the persons behind the action. She is committing to bless those people as a fellow image-bearers, to give them the benefit of the doubt, and to call out the good in them even if they themselves cannot see it.

We tell better stories to help the hurting reclaim their dignity.

We tell better stories to soften our hearts.

We tell better stories because we know that no one comes into the world angry, careless, and callous. Something helped them get there. We will not add insult to injury by treating them as if that's all they are—wounded animals on the side of the road.

We tell better stories because we believe the best story: God's love and redemption for all who are hurting.

Whenever I talk to people about this practice of telling better stories, I always hear the same response: "Well, what about Hitler? He doesn't deserve a better story. Look at what he did!" And I agree that image-bearers can do terrible things. But Shalom Sistas decide to tell better stories about our enemies, because we believe the image of God can never be completely erased from a person. Blurred, yes, but never erased.

When I think of people who do despicable things, I think of a graffiti flower.

There was a wall I loved to pass by in Cambridge that was sanctioned by the city as a legal place for graffiti. Nearly every week new art popped up, often covering the art that was once there. The wall was just a few feet away from my favorite Thai restaurant, and on my way to lunch with a friend one day, I saw a beautiful flower on the wall. It was pink with a yellow center. It was so realistic that it seemed as though I could grab it directly from the wall.

The next time I walked by, however, I saw that someone had painted over the stem. A few weeks later when I visited the wall, you could only see the corner of the topmost petal. A few months later, I couldn't see it at all. I knew it was there, I longed to see it again, but it was covered over by layers and layers of spray paint.

If I could have done so, I would have scrubbed away at those layers to get back to the flower. This is what a Shalom Sista does when she chooses to tell better stories: she scrubs away at the layers of bitterness, pain, and hurt to see the beauty.

Sometimes this looks like researching the person we dislike the most—the angry politician, the church leader caught in impropriety, the friend who betrayed us—to learn what might have caused the hurt. If we do not have the luxury of knowing someone's painful backstory, we use our own imaginations to create one. The point isn't to get the details right. The point is to have a change of heart.

The point is to become better storytellers.

One of my favorite examples of telling a better story about our enemies—or anyone who is just beyond our empathy—comes from Dr. Martin Luther King Jr. King was in a march for civil rights in the Deep South when a group of white men flanked his group and began yelling, spitting, and physically attacking them.

Mind you, only the day before, King had been released from a county jail after being arrested for marching. He was weary both emotionally and physically, and now he was being attacked for standing up against the brokenness of this world.

As a young white man screamed in his face, King waited for him to take a breath, and then he said, "Young man. You are too good-looking and smart to have such hate in your heart."

That's a better story, isn't it? King could have called him a racist, or even argued history and law with him. But no—he called out the image of God in that young man and cast a vision of wholeness for that man to live into.

That's the power we have, Sistas! We are kingdom storytellers. When the world rages against us, we gracefully control the narrative. The stories we tell are always, always in line with the heart of God. While our enemies' actions are not good, the potential for good rests within them. We tell them that they're not too far gone; they've simply lost their way back home. But we know the way back home, don't we? I want to be the kind of woman whose stories are signposts of hope on the way back to the kingdom: signposts for everyone—even my enemies, especially intense moms in the carpool lane.

I haven't seen Jeep Driver in a while. My kids think she was maybe a visiting aunt or something. That would explain the meltdown—out-of-towners do not handle our driving shenanigans well. At. All.

But every afternoon, right around pickup time, I pick out a book to read in case I have to sit for a bit, waiting in line—like I'm supposed to. On the way out of the house, I grab my purse and my keys, and I pray a little prayer: "Jesus, help me tell better stories, help me tell better stories, help me tell better stories. Oh—and may the odds be ever in my favor."

Amen.

-11-

Shalom with a Swiffer: We Will Serve before We Speak

A noble leader answers not to the trumpet calls of self promotion, but to the hushed whispers of necessity.
—Mollie Marti

I have a special tenderness for new mamas and their families. It's true. Just about every Sunday morning, I'm looking for the new mamas at church—to welcome them back, to offer to hold their babies, or to wipe their toddler's face. I love them so much. They're brave and beautiful and incredibly thoughtful—even when they themselves don't feel that way. They are curious and intense in all the best ways. If not for a few experienced mamas who came alongside me and told me all the good they saw in me when I felt my worst—Mentor Moms at Cambridgeport Baptist Church, I'm looking at you—I don't know where I would be.

So, as a mother of older children, I get to be a cheerleader for new mamas. If you have small ones, I have two things to tell you.

1. You're killing it. Even if you don't feel it, you are. Your baby is fed and loved.
2. It does get better. Not easier, because motherhood is the constant pouring of yourself into fragile little vessels, and that is never easy. But it will get better. The exhaustion will go away, and they'll start talking and laughing and becoming little people who you kinda love to have around.

So don't give up. And if you're local, call me! I'll hold that baby or take the little ones to the park to give you a couple of hours of peace. When it's time to pass those kiddos back to you, I'll tell you that a messy bun and yoga pants is so your look. You are slaying mommy chic.

This deep love for new mamas has made me a great support. It has also caused quite a few instances of, shall we say, forceful enthusiasm.

Okay, bossiness.

I can get really bossy when I talk to new moms. There's this pride in me that threatens to edge out my adoration for new families, and I'm constantly trying to keep it in check. It does make sense that I would feel like an authority on new motherhood, since I mothered two babies in one year. You might even call me an "older woman" in your Titus 2 ministry. I know all the tips, tricks, products, and magazines, and I'm just itching to tell new moms what they need to survive this overwhelming season.

While my experience and passion combine to make me a potentially great leader in a moms' group, I had a season during which I turned down invitations to speak and lead simply because my heart was not in a good place. I was overly eager to show my knowledge and hear praise. I noticed that as my enthusiasm to give advice grew, so did my propensity for offense if my amazingly sage and perfect advice was not received well. Shalom for others at the expense of ourselves rarely brings the goodness of the kingdom of God down to earth. So for almost a year, even though my kids were eleven, eight, and seven and I solidly fit into that "mentor mom" category, I chose to serve new mamas before I spoke into their lives. It was my promise to marry humility with peacemaking.

A word about humility. When we begin to conceptualize our shalom practices in the world, there is a deep hole of introspection that we can stumble into as we think through all the facets of service. Whom should I serve? When? For how long? Why? And the most prominent stumbling block for me: What do other people think of me?

The commitment to serve before we speak clears the path for us. This manifesto point means we're beginning the process of thinking about others' needs, experiences, and preferences before our own.

Humility is not putting yourself down or ignoring your own needs. Humility serves as a neutralizer for our egos. By thinking less of ourselves, we create space and energy to think of others.

This manifesto point—We will serve before we speak—is not questioning the appropriateness of women to serve in leadership or the call of the church to speak out about justice. It is our promise to align ourselves with a posture of humility as we do those things. It's a third way of viewing servanthood that combines our great awareness of what we have to offer the world with an other-centered focus.

Serving before we speak is our commitment to training ourselves to move through the world as students of the brokenhearted. Serving before we speak means that we can seek their wholeness with authenticity and kindness.

When we worked in the urban core, I was often frustrated by church or community groups who would sign up to "serve" with us . . . but never consult the director of the community center to find out what we needed. They would show up with curriculum and snacks and an itinerary for their time in the city. Then when they left, we'd have more problems and things to clean up: an abundance of resources we couldn't use because they were irrelevant to kids in the hood, kids who expected to be taken to an amusement park the next week just as they had with "the people in the orange shirts." Our staff soon became exhausted from playing tour guide to visiting do-gooders.

I've heard stories of mission groups that bring materials to build wells . . . only to find out the village couldn't sustain one or the people lacked the basic tools to build, like hammers and screwdrivers.

What if we ask, "How can we support what you're already doing?" Serving before we speak gives us an opportunity to create wholeness in a lasting way, not just in the ways that give us a momentary thrill as benefactors of the "poor."

Nadia Bolz-Weber, pastor of House for All Sinners and Saints in Denver, Colorado, and author of *Accidental Saints*, warns us to remember that although we are called to bless the poor, we are not the blessing! "While we as people of God are certainly called to feed the hungry and clothe the naked, that whole 'we're blessed to be a blessing' thing can still be kind of dangerous," she writes. "It can be dangerous when we self-importantly place ourselves above the world, waiting to descend on those below so we can be the 'blessing' they've been waiting for, like it or not."

If we don't learn to serve before we speak, we will be in danger of missing the point of our peacemaking. That's what happened when the sons of Zebedee approached Jesus with an outrageous request.

* * *

The disciples were arguing about who was the greatest.

> Jesus said to them, "The kings of the Gentiles lord it over them; and those who exercise authority over them call themselves Benefactors. But you are not to be like that. Instead, the greatest among you should be like the youngest, and the one who rules like the one who serves. For who is greater, the one who is at the table or the one who serves? Is it not the one who is at the table? But I am among you as one who serves. You are those who have stood by me in my trials. And I confer on you a kingdom, just as my Father conferred one on me, so that you may eat and drink at my table in my kingdom." (Luke 22:25-30)

For context, right before this teaching on leadership and serv-anthood in the kingdom of God, two disciples asked Jesus for a favor. More specifically, their mama asked for a favor. (Lord help me not be a pushy mama for my boys. Thank you and amen.) She, the mother of John and James, often called the sons of Zebedee, asked: When your kingdom comes, will you appoint my two sons on your left and right?

Jesus warned them that they did not know what they were asking. He knew that his kingdom would come on the cross. As Brian Zahnd says, "The cross is the coronation of the world's rightful King."

That's not exactly what John and James—or their mama—had in mind. Even though they had walked with Jesus for nearly three years, the disciples were still a little confused about what the king-dom of God meant and how Jesus was going to inaugurate it. They were still working with an earthly framework of "power over" authority—violence, dominance, mutiny—while Jesus sought to introduce them to the "power under" way of heaven—selfless love, subversion, unity. Since they had this framework, their idea of suc-cessful leaders would be the ones who led from the top down, which explains their ask.

Jesus' response was to ask them if they truly knew that which they asked. Then he turned them down, sparking a heated debate among the disciples. Who, in fact, was the greatest among them? Again, Jesus highlighted the differences between an earthly power-over leadership and the kingdom's power-under leadership. In the kingdom, we lead as we come under those in need and offer our service.

As Shalom Sistas, we recognize that we are uniquely gifted to bring about God's shalom here on earth. We take to heart Fred-erick Buechner's words on calling: "By and large a good rule for finding out is this: the kind of work God usually calls you to is the kind of work (a) that you need most to do and (b) that the world most needs to have done. . . . The place God calls you to is the place where your deep gladness and the world's deep hunger meet."

But it's equally important for us to enter into the place God calls us to with the same humility as Jesus, who "though he was God, . . . did not think of equality with God as something to cling to" (Philippians 2:6 NLT).

When we are moved by a great need—an unreached people group, a village suffering from the HIV/AIDS epidemic, a community with lead in their water, a neighborhood riddled with gang violence, an exhausted mama—we tend to want to lead from the top down. We are the expert, or the most-resourced, or the one with the gospel, or the one with the right connections. So we (unintentionally) lord it over those we serve: with our five steps toward fundraising, an article written by our favorite theologian, the subtle insertion of our agenda because we've footed the bill, and so many other ways of undermining our acts of peace for communities in turmoil. When we forget that to be an effective leader in the kingdom of God is to be an adept servant, our helping can hurt the very ones we're called to serve.

So while I love babies like a pro—I can sing lullabies, change diapers, wrap a baby burrito, and snap a pic to text to the mama to reassure her while she's away—it means nothing if I don't have humility. Humility—serving before speaking—is essential if I want to be a shalom practitioner and not just a really gifted babysitter.

* * *

When I was younger, my daddy and I would play chess and plan my future.

Daddy moves his white pawn to E4. "So, when you get to high school you're going to need to hit the extracurriculars really hard, like debate team and foreign language club."

I move my black pawn to E5. "Which foreign language?"

Dad's bishop to D6. "Any will do; preferably Spanish, since we're in Texas."

"I wanna learn French," I say as I move my pawn to F4.

He shrugs and takes my pawn. "Like I said, any will do. Don't give up your pawns too soon in the game, Osheta. You'll need them later. Have you figured out what type of law you want to study? You could be a public defender, since you have a soft heart for people in need."

I stare at the board, planning my next move; I so desperately want to impress him. Not seeing a way to capture his piece, I decide to have fun with the game. I move my knight to H3 just because I love to make him jump over the pawns to get to his place.

"No, not yet. I'll figure that out when I get to college. I'll just stick to the plan and make captain of the debate team for my senior year, okay? When I get into a good school, we'll figure that out."

Daddy moves a pawn to G5 and nods. "That's fine."

I can see that he's going after my knight, and part of me feels that he's doing it just to ruin my fun. "Daddy, sometimes I get called 'white' because of our plan for me go to college and become a lawyer."

My knight takes his audacious pawn. I catch his eye and he smirks. I wonder if he moved that piece there just so I'd take it and have a moment of victory in our little game.

"Sheeki"—this is my childhood nickname—"don't listen to those fools! Just remember this: When you come back from school with your degree and your high-paying job, you can hire them to clean your house and take care of your kids. They'll be coming to you, begging for work and saying, 'Remember when we were kids?' So let them say what they want now. Someday you'll be signing their paychecks."

This was my daddy's version of "Haters are going to hate." During our chess games, he strategically wove in me a sense of pride and expectation about my future leadership: one day I was going to acquire a successful career and make lots of money.

One day I was going to be the boss.

* * *

Which is why several years ago, on the morning that I decided to take my kids to work with me, I despaired.

It was Take Our Daughters and Sons to Work Day. As we were packing up for the day, my daughter, who shares my love for babies and eagerness to help in the nursery, asked, "Do you take care of a family's baby, Mama?"

When I told her no, she asked why. I didn't know what to say, so I gave some pat answer about wanting to help the family where they really needed it. Plus, they already had a nanny.

Instead of being the nanny, a position where I would have shone and led with confidence, I was the housekeeper.

As we drove in the snow to Kathleen's home, I worried that I was letting my dad down. I wasn't taking my kids to an office with a view; I was taking them to another family's apartment to work through a chore list.

I couldn't show off the perks of free coffee and pastries in the breakroom; all I had to show was a house key that proved I had earned a family's trust.

I didn't sit my children down around an imposing conference table with impressive colleagues; I taught them how to intuit a family's need. ("Fold down the top sheet, because it's super comfy to get into a well-made bed"; "Wipe under the glass of the coffee table to make it shine"; "Fold the clothes a bit neater, 'k?")

That day, my kids did not see me in an illustrious career as a lawyer, or even my noble secondary choice of teacher. Instead I took them to help me with my Tuesday-and-Thursday gig of housekeeping for the sweetest, kindest young family.

I, their black mama, took them to the home of a white family. To clean.

Was I harming my children more than helping them by letting them watch me work? Should they see me in such a menial role? What messages was I sending them about the world and their worth as biracial children? What did it say about my worth as a black woman?

In a culture in which every little black girl looks up to Michelle Obama and every Thursday evening we're blown away by Olivia

Pope, I wondered if I was throwing away the liberties afforded me by the civil rights movement. Sometimes I felt a deep, deep shame when I thought about my choice to become a housekeeper.

I'm a black woman. We've evolved from this, haven't we?

Deciding whether to bring my kids to work with me that day, I questioned my rejection of my father's carefully thought-out plan and my lack of motivation to go to law school.

That is, until I unlocked the door.

I stood there, surveying the apartment, and I realized there's a subversive beauty to being a housekeeper—even a black housekeeper for a white family.

Hold on. Hear me out.

That day, as my children worked beside me, I sensed a deeper purpose than teaching a strong work ethic. I thought of Jesus modeling servanthood, strategically teaching his disciples the greatest values of the kingdom—the first shall be last and the last first. I knew how to answer my daughter. I cleaned houses because Jesus was strategically teaching me to be last when I wanted to be first.

With every instruction to my children to thoughtfully care for this family's home as if our own, I told a new story about race and roles. As Jesus-followers, we know that there is no Jew nor Greek. There is no room for racism. We seek respect and unity for all people.

I also told them a new story about leadership and servanthood—Jesus, our Lord, came to serve and not be served.

With pictures of this lovely family surrounding us, I explained how Kathleen wanted to do all these things herself but she had to work outside the house. I told them how exhausting it is to come home from work and have to cook a meal and take care of a baby. So their mama comes in to help.

Their mama comes in to help.

Yes, their mama was "the help." There it was again. My daddy's strategic chess game conversations flooded back, forcing me to parse through a miasma of shame. Conventional knowledge said I should be ashamed of myself, maybe even remorseful for not actualizing my potential.

What should I do with the fact that, in truth, I actually loved being the help?

I loved it because, for two days a week, I could simply love people outside my family with my hands. I got to extend grace over their mess and to practice shalom with a Swiffer.

Some may say it's degrading to get a to-do list of chores, but that's only true if I allow it to be. I only feel degraded by my choice to be a housekeeper when my pride makes me forget the teachings of Jesus, the wise rabbi who strategically modeled the bedrock ethics of the kingdom: humility, hospitality, love.

> When he had finished washing their feet, he put on his clothes and returned to his place. "Do you understand what I have done for you?" he asked them. "You call me 'Teacher' and 'Lord,' and rightly so, for that is what I am. Now that I, your Lord and Teacher, have washed your feet, you also should wash one another's feet. I have set you an example that you should do as I have done for you. Very truly I tell you, no servant is greater than his master, nor is a messenger greater than the one who sent him. Now that you know these things, you will be blessed if you do them." (John 13:12-17)

We don't wash feet anymore. Our culture says that serving, when we have the capacity to lead, is beneath us. At the least, it's a waste of our potential. But Jesus said to the group of leaders he was grooming to start a revolution that, in his kingdom, "You ought to wash each other's feet" (v. 14 NLT).

If we don't get this, then we have no part of our Servant King, Jesus. Simon Peter got it, which is why he said, "Then, Lord . . . not just my feet but my hands and my head as well!" (John 13:9). He was eager to embody this truth, and when I serve before I speak, so am I. I get to embody this teaching by doing someone else's least favorite chores. Twice a week during those years I humbled myself to the lowest position in their household's structure. Twice a week I felt connected to Jesus in a profound way.

* * *

To this day, my kids remember when I brought them with me when I worked as a housekeeper. Sometimes I still wonder if I should give them something more impressive to aspire to. I mean, I do want them to go to college and move out.

But even more than that, I want them to remember that Mama asked "How can I love?" before she asked "How much does it pay?" I want them to learn to ask "How can I serve?" before they ask "How can I rise to the top?"

As strategic as my daddy's chess games and plans for future success were, I believe that inviting my children to clean house with me taught them something about the kingdom's economy of love. As we cleaned side by side, I showed them that sometimes love looks like sparkling Formica and hard-boiled eggs.

By practicing shalom with a Swiffer, I hope that I dusted away some of the shame of not achieving career success or impressive "mentor mom" leadership. By serving before I speak, I hope I help my children learn that we can live out the humility of the kingdom of God, right here and right now.

Serving before you speak is subversive, and it's strategic. But, you know, so is Jesus.

-12-

Jesus' Party Planners: We Will Build Bridges, Not Walls

We are each other's harvest; we are each other's business; we are each other's magnitude and bond.
—Gwendolyn Brooks

Longsuffering and brave Sistas with tween girls in your homes: come close, for we must hold each other. Some of us have been yelled at by our girls, just this past hour. Some have had doors slammed in our faces. Some of us are holding this book with damp hands straight from drawing baths for our daughters who are battling self-hate because boys are clueless and *Cosmo* in the checkout line is straight-up pernicious.

And some of us, including me, have just coaxed a crying girl out of her heartbreak. Let us hold one another and whisper soft, sweet things: You will survive. She didn't mean to call you a grubby witch. This too shall pass . . . hopefully.

Recently, my daughter was bawling into my pillow because I told her she could not go to her school's daddy-daughter dance. Every spring our elementary school has two big fundraising events: the daddy-daughter dance and the mother-son Olympics. Coming from a highly inclusive school in Cambridge, I thought it was odd to make these events the centerpiece of the school's spring calendar. But I didn't want to be a progressive snob, so I let it slide . . . until last year, when my daughter brought home the invitation and begged to go.

At that time, we couldn't afford new school shoes for the kids, so a forty-five-dollar ticket to a dance in a school gym was simply out of the question. It broke my heart to say no, but I did, and off she went to cry into her pillow.

Always willing to give time when I don't have the money, I called the director and offered to help in exchange for a discounted ticket. I would be thrilled to join the organizing committee, I said, and I even have a background in event planning. Parties are kinda my secret obsession. (After reading this book you may think peace-making is, but no. It's parties. All day. Every day. I love confetti, and color-coordinated paper goods, and balloons, and curated playlists. All you have to do is give me a budget and an excuse.)

I once threw a rock-star "unbirthday" party for all three of my kids in the spring, because their birthdays are back-to-back in the fall and they always overwhelm me. I made up for skipping their actual birthdays with a "tour bus" (my van decorated with their names, snacks to the kids' specifications, and me in a chauffeur hat), a concert at the local library by their favorite band, and a scavenger hunt—all for less than $200. So, you know, I had ideas and energy for this daddy-daughter party.

I was told no. They were not interested in accepting outside help. The ticket prices were what they were, and if we couldn't come, well, they were very sorry.

Even though I was disappointed, I completely got it. The event was a fundraiser, after all! They couldn't just hand out tickets to everyone, or else they wouldn't make money for the school. On the other hand, setting the ticket price higher than a tank of gas creates an unnecessary obstacle for low-income students.

So this year, when the daddy-daughter dance flyer came, and we could afford to send Trinity and T. C., we had to give it a second look before investing in the evening. On that second look, it became clear to me that T. C. and I were slightly uncomfortable with the concept of the dance. Daddy-daughter dances and the idea of "dating your daughter" have been a popular trend in some churches we've attended in the past. It's a noble movement, on one hand: the church recognizes the impact a father has on his daughter and wants to equip their men (who are often celebrated for leadership within their families but not always empowered to be vulnerable and tender) with opportunities to spend time with their daughters.

But the idea of daddy-daughter dances gets sticky real fast. Historically, men would bring their daughters to dances to show them to the other men in the town with one of two goals: to display "property" that validated their status, or to show off property "for sale" (in other words, available for marriage) to the strongest candidate. Also, traditionally, men do not buy flowers for and slow dance with women they are not interested in sexually or romantically.

We deeply believe that image-bearers are not property to show off or profit from. Men respect women, including their daughters, by getting to know them for their minds, their character, and what they contribute to the world, not for their bodies. The dance didn't quite fit within our framework as a family seeking shalom. So when I asked my husband to take our daughter to the dance, he said, emphatically, "No."

When I told my daughter this, she appealed to my ego and said, "But, Mom, you and Dad don't have to worry about this. I know God made me good and men are supposed to be good to women. You guys always talk to me about that. I just wanna go to spend time with Dad and make memories."

Well, how can you argue with that?

We decided to give the dance the benefit of the doubt. T. C. and I looked at the budget to see if we could afford the ticket price (this year it was thirty-five dollars per daddy-daughter couple, plus ten dollars for every additional daughter). Still steep, but doable for us.

I was sitting down to write the check when I noticed a knot in my stomach and unshed tears in my eyes, clouding my view of the check. I personally knew of a few families who could not afford to go. Trinity had just told me about a little girl who ran off during lunch time to cry because her father was not in the picture and she didn't know if she could go to the dance. As I filled out the check, I kept thinking about that girl and other students like her: What about the kids who cannot attend? Does this event reinforce exclusion? Why isn't there a way for all students to be a part of the dance?

As Shalom Sistas, we are responsible for thinking about people on the margins, just as Jesus did. In this case, it was all the daddy-daughter pairs who would miss the dance because their finances didn't allow it. I couldn't shake the conviction that this was an opportunity to practice shalom for the school—before sending Trinity to the dance there was something I needed to do.

I contacted the dance organizers and offered to pay an amount above my daughter's ticket toward a scholarship fund. Or if the committee didn't want to oversee a scholarship fund, I asked, would they help me find families who might not be able to afford the dance so that we could help offset the cost of their tickets?

I received an email almost immediately. Even though they knew the cost of the dance was an issue, they had done all they could to reduce the price. Scholarships or other ways to create opportunities for students to come were just not a priority for the planning committee.

"It's very kind of you," the email read, "but no." Immediately, I knew the source of my discomfort: if we sent Trinity we would be contributing to the wall of division on campus that the dance was building. As a Shalom Sista, I just couldn't do it, so I had to have a hard conversation with my tween girl.

* * *

This manifesto point—We will build bridges, not walls—is an act of resistance to division. We live in a world that avoids discomfort at all costs. We curate our lives so that we hear, see, and interact with people just like us. It's not that we *want* to be divisive; it's just in the air we breathe.

Listen: if a friend posts online that she thinks Beyoncé is the worst performer of all time and that Taylor Swift deserves to win all the VMAs forever and ever amen, I have to sit alone with Jesus until I overcome the impulse to drive directly to her house and make her listen to "Run the World (Girls)" on repeat.

There's a psychological concept called cognitive dissonance that comes into play here. Cognitive dissonance occurs when, for example, what we believe to be true is challenged by someone we love who holds a different perspective. At that point we're faced with the dilemma of holding both ideas in tension. Some people feel actual pain as their brains attempt to form new grooves to make space for new ideas, which is why cognitive dissonance is categorized as a form of mental stress. When this occurs, we can wrestle with these new ideas, or we can stop the process by rejecting the person and avoiding him or her.

This is one of the reasons why, when my husband and I have an argument, I can feel pressure in my head. That's cognitive dissonance.

The same is true for other relationships in my life. When I have to interact with people I have categorized as different from me, I sometimes try to avoid them altogether, because their very presence produces cognitive dissonance. This is why I look away when I see homeless people on the side of the road. Their poverty is meeting my affluence in a deeply disquieting way. On the other hand, this is also why I struggle with hanging out at the school bake sale. The moms at my kids' schools, with their stories of botched fifty-dollar gel manicures and weekend trips to their cabins in Big Bear, meet my social justice-y, strive-to-give-everything-up-for-the-poor self.

Sometimes in these encounters, my brain actually hurts. (Also, since we're friends here, jealousy is a fantastic fire starter for cognitive dissonance. That's a bit of what goes on at the bake sale.)

I had to wrestle with this cognitive dissonance before I could actively begin building a bridge on a playdate one autumn afternoon in Boston.

$*$ $*$ $*$

Among mothers, there is a certain playdate etiquette. We adhere to it whenever our children rush up to us and beg, "Mom, can [insert name of new Best Friend Forever] come over and play?"

When the new child arrives at our house, we don't offer peanut products of any kind, in any configuration, in any amount. Ever. Even if the child has peanut butter smudges across her chin and brags about all the Reese's Pieces she got on Halloween night. Never. Because just your luck, the moment you serve that baby a PB&J, her latent nut allergy will manifest and she'll go into anaphylactic shock right on your kitchen floor. Better safe than sorry. So no nuts. What I started doing is making good old-fashioned toast with fun spreads: honey and bananas, cream cheese and lavender honey, assorted jams, and fun butters. (Yes, girl, butter can be fun. And fatty. But our bodies are wholly good, so let's not yuck each other's yum. Find some recipes on pages 233–34.)

Over the course of the playdate, I monitor screen time, make sure any homework is completed, and of course, observe the most important of playdate etiquette: a chat with the mother at the pickup for at least twenty minutes over tea, water, coffee, or in my favorite cases, snacks.

Snacks not withstanding, I usually dread this part of the playdate. I mean, really, what do we have to talk about after I update her on our afternoon? There was lots of reading. Lots of Legos. Lots of noise. Not a single nut in sight. Then we sit in an awkward silence until one of us mentions having to make dinner and rushes our children out the door under a frenzied cloud of thank yous and promises to do this again.

I always feel at a loss during these conversations, which is exactly how I felt when Laura came over to pick up her son one autumn afternoon a few years ago.

I was especially nervous about our post-playdate conversation, because just days before, I had found out she was a lesbian. Can you believe it? A lesbian!?! Like, with an actual partner at home! I'm embarrassed to admit I was worried about sending my son to her house, so when she suggested I host the playdate because she had class that afternoon, I was relieved.

Laura, with her gregarious, no-nonsense personality, firm handshake, and well-worn North Face fleece, was the stereotype I feared. Oh, the thoughts I, the evangelical Christian, thought about Laura, the liberal, godless, angry, skeptical, feminist lesbian.

At pickup, I offered Laura coffee, and she agreed, since the boys were in the middle of creating the biggest leaf pile of all time and needed just "ten more minutes, Moms!"

Holding my cup of coffee with both hands, I asked, "So what class did you just come from?"

"Life of Jesus. I'm almost finished with my program at the Episcopal Divinity School," Laura said.

Interest sparked and thoroughly confused, I asked, "So are you planning on becoming a what . . . a priest? Like with the Episcopal Church?"

Laura gave me a knowing smile over her cup as she took a sip. She nodded, and went on to tell me her story. She told me about setting up her stuffed animals as a little girl and serving them Holy Communion. She confessed to struggling as a young woman to reconcile her calling and sexuality. She shared how every day in her seminary program, she felt as though she were coming home. She got to talk about Jesus all day and then show his love to her parishioners in the evenings.

While listening to her story, I whispered in my soul, "Lord, do we have more in common than I think?" Here was this woman, as different from me as one could be: Her midforties to my late twenties. Her short salt-and-pepper bob to my chemically relaxed ponytail. Her white skin to my brown. Her gay to my straight. Yet we had one person in common.

Jesus.

I told her about how T. C. and I were sensing God calling us to plant a church and how I had so many fears. I had been out of the urban ministry life for so long that I worried that I wouldn't authentically connect with our new church. I was still a girl from a suburb in love with the city, I said, and that chasm always feels too much for me to cross.

Laura then asked if she could pray with me. With our heads bowed, she placed her hands on my shoulders and talked to Jesus . . . about me. For me. With tears caught in her throat, she reminded me of God's faithfulness in a benediction. It humbled me.

Completely.

As we prayed, that sweet, generous, barrier-breaking presence of Jesus was palpable. Jesus was right there standing on the porch with us, the feminist lesbian priest-to-be and a well-meaning but still judgmental evangelical urban missionary.

Right there, with boys giggling in the background and colorful leaves swirling around our feet, Jesus challenged my stereotypes and undermined my legalism. When we said amen together, I felt the Holy Spirit whisper back to me. Conviction gripped my heart. I was guilty of building a wall, when I should have been building a bridge.

Jesus changes everything. Whatever I may have felt about Laura's sexual orientation or her calling, I knew one thing about her. Laura loved Jesus as much as I did. That one piece of information was all I needed to reach out my hand and call her my sister.

* * *

It's always startling when I realize the walls I've put up against those who seem different from me. The construction of those walls starts with my language about the other person. They're always wrong or godless, clueless or backward. Then it continues with my behavior: I stand away from them, I watch them out of the corner of my eye, or I hold my breath when they pass in expectation that they are going to offend me. Even though I know that Jesus, on the cross, broke down the enmity that makes me want to build walls instead of building bridges.

Paul says it this way in Ephesians:

> For he himself is our peace, who has made the two groups one and has destroyed the barrier, the dividing wall of hostility, by setting aside in his flesh the law with its commands and regulations. His purpose was to create in himself one new humanity out of the two, thus making peace, and in one body to reconcile both of them to God through the cross, by which he put to death their hostility. He came and preached peace to you who were far away and peace to those who were near. For through him we both have access to the Father by one Spirit.
>
> Consequently, you are no longer foreigners and strangers, but fellow citizens with God's people and also members of his household, built on the foundation of the apostles and prophets, with Christ Jesus himself as the chief cornerstone. In him the whole building is joined together and rises to become a holy temple in the Lord. And in him you too are being built together to become a dwelling in which God lives by his Spirit. (Ephesians 2:14-22)

After we acknowledge our cognitive dissonance, we can decide to press through to find things we have in common with someone else instead of obsessing about the ways we're different. As Shalom Sistas, we are tasked with the work of actively building bridges.

And for me, if I'mma cross a treacherous bridge for the sake of reconciliation, there better be cake on the other end.

There better be a party.

* * *

Jesus was a terrific troublemaker, yes. But one of the things I love most about him is that he was a fantastic partier too. Jesus attended so many parties (invited or not) that a rumor went around that he was a drunkard and a glutton (see Matthew 11:19 and Luke 7:34). As one pastor put it, "Whenever people couldn't find Jesus, they'd just ask, 'Who's having a party?' and there they would find him."

Jesus routinely built bridges between people, and the way we see this most clearly is by looking at whom Jesus spent his time with, whom he ate with, and whom he partied with. Jesus would eat and celebrate with anyone—tax collectors, Pharisees, prostitutes, zealots —and everyone. He was indiscriminate with this attendance.

One could even argue that some of Jesus' best teachings were at parties.

Jesus loved to go to parties, but he also had a reputation for not having the best party etiquette. He would point out the biases of those in attendance, often to expose the walls they had built and to reveal the bridge-building heart of God. When I think about Jesus at parties, I think about my mama's favorite warning to us when we'd go out in public: "Don't you dare act a fool!"

"Don't act a fool" meant you had better be on your best behavior. Follow all the rules and use all your social graces. Do not stick your fingers in the ground meat, or interrupt when adults are talking, or pinch your sister because she stuck her tongue out at you, or run around screaming just to hear the echo in the aisles, or stick your grubby hands in Mama's purse to get a quarter for the gumball machine, or other nonsense. Basically, it was our warning: "Don't you dare embarrass Mama when you're out in the world with her."

I really wonder what Mary's version of "Don't act a fool" was for Jesus. Whatever it was, I don't think Jesus paid attention to it, because our Lord routinely acted a fool for the kingdom. Which makes complete sense, because "God chose the foolish things of the world to shame the wise" (1 Corinthians 1:27).

There's one party in particular that I love to think about when I want to practice bridge building. It's found in Luke. One Sabbath, Jesus was eating at the house of a prominent Pharisee when his lousy party etiquette went on display.

There in front of him was a man suffering from abnormal swelling of his body. Jesus asked the Pharisees and experts in the law, "Is it lawful to heal on the Sabbath or not?" But they remained silent. So taking hold of the man, he healed him and sent him on his way.

Then he asked them, "If one of you has a child or an ox that falls into a well on the Sabbath day, will you not immediately pull it out?" And they had nothing to say.

When he noticed how the guests picked the places of honor at the table, he told them this parable: "When someone invites you to a wedding feast, do not take the place of honor, for a person more distinguished than you may have been invited. If so, the host who invited both of you will come and say to you, 'Give this person your seat.' Then, humiliated, you will have to take the least important place. But when you are invited, take the lowest place, so that when your host comes, he will say to you, 'Friend, move up to a better place.' Then you will be honored in the presence of all the other guests. For all those who exalt themselves will be humbled, and those who humble themselves will be exalted."

Then Jesus said to his host, "When you give a luncheon or dinner, do not invite your friends, your brothers or sisters, your relatives, or your rich neighbors; if you do, they may invite you back and so you will be repaid. But when you give a banquet, invite the poor, the crippled, the lame, the blind, and you will be blessed. Although they cannot repay you, you will be repaid at the resurrection of the righteous." (Luke 14:2-14)

Jesus had been invited to this dinner by a Pharisee. Now, we have already talked about the Pharisees—they were the religious people of the day. Your pastors, your Sunday school teachers, your fellowship team leaders, the deaconesses—you get the idea. This particular meal was on the Sabbath, so this was essentially Sunday dinner. If there is one thing I've learned over twenty years in the church, it's that you don't act a fool at Sunday dinner. And yet . . . Jesus did, and by doing so, he gave us a clear direction on how we should embody the bridge-building ethic of the kingdom of God.

First, he healed a man right at the dinner table, which was a violation of the Sabbath. Then Jesus, undeterred, went on to correct the dinner guests about their gathering etiquette—in particular, who sits where and who is invited.

You know that thing we like to do when we're out in a group and we're excited about talking with some of the people but not with others? We sit next to the people we know so we can (a) have comfortable conversations, (b) impress, or (c) network in order to get ahead. Jesus noticed this tendency, and after he healed a man so many people at the table had ignored, he used their avoidance as a teaching moment for how they could better embody the kingdom act of building bridges.

Picture this with me: Jesus went up into this Pharisee's own home, sat down at his table, ate his food, drank his wine, and then proceeded to tell him he was doing the whole hospitality thing all wrong. As my son T. J. would say, that Pharisee got roasted.

Because we take our cues from Jesus, Shalom Sistas ask, "Am I building a wall where there should be a bridge?" If so, we need the courage to learn from people with different perspectives and the conviction to challenge systems that create divisions.

* * *

When we told Trinity she could not go to the daddy-daughter dance because it was exclusionary—both for girls who did not have father figures in their lives and for those who could not afford it—she ran off to cry. Understandably. She likes my bedroom, because I have the best pillows in the house. It's true. They're perfect for both sleeping and ugly crying. Which we had a lot of that afternoon.

I told her to cry all she wanted to. Let it out. But when she was ready to talk, I had an idea. And so I lay down next to her on our bed and waited while my poor girl cried for nearly thirty minutes.

Sometimes our commitment to build bridges will cost us. It takes more resources, time, and courage to build bridges instead of walls. Did you know that in construction, you can build a wall in under two days, while a bridge takes anywhere from one year to four? Bridge building is a hard, long undertaking. It always starts with a costly decision, one that we know will hurt. But we are women of the cross—we are empowered by the Holy Spirit to create wholeness by breaking down walls and resisting division.

"Okay, Mom," she finally croaked, as the sobbing subsided. "What's your idea?"

I read her the passage from Luke and made jokes about Jesus acting up for the sake of the kingdom. I told her about building bridges.

Then I asked, "What if we threw a party the night of the dance? It can be any kind of party you'd like. And we could do what Jesus said: we can invite everyone and anyone."

Trinity started talking about the kids in her school, listing the names of people she could invite.

The girl whose dad was absent? Invited!

The friend whose parents were in a bitter conflict and she has been caught in the emotional crossfire? Invited!

The boys who didn't understand why they couldn't have a night of dancing too? Invited!

"Everyone can come to our party! That's what we'll call the party, 'Everybody come'!" Trinity announced, voice clearer, stronger, and more resolved than it had been a few minutes earlier.

"Yes, baby," I said. "Everybody come."

I shared about our "Everybody come" party on Facebook, and a surprising thing happened: Women started offering to send money to help pay for the party. Sistas sent encouraging words for Trinity to continue standing up for inclusion, even when it hurts. Friends and acquaintances left voicemail messages offering prayer, and several sent donations for pizza, a DJ, and decorations.

We were floored.

You see, there's a benefit to bridge building that we often forget. Sure, building bridges is ego-breaking and brain-hurting work, but it's also deeply relational. Building bridges creates a pathway for people from different backgrounds, perspectives, and cultures to move freely in each other's lives. You share a prayer need. I share a victory. You share a recipe. I share a joke. You send your baby over for a playdate. I make toast and pray we don't need Benadryl. Together, we as shalom practitioners build bridges and not walls to reveal the unique quality of the kingdom of God.

Everyone's invited. Everybody come to the party. There's room on the dance floor for us all.

PART V

Shalom in Our World

-13-

Love Bombs: We Will Choose Ordinary Acts of Peace

Don't be overwhelmed, it's not our calling to save the world. Do what you can. Do it well. Do it with love.
  —Eugene Cho

Babers! Quick! Come here!" T. C. called me from the other room. I ran up the stairs of our Cambridge townhome and stuck my head in our bedroom. My husband was sitting on the bed, reading something on his computer. "What do you think about Los Angeles?" he asked.

"I don't know," I said. "Why?" I called over my shoulder before turning to head back downstairs.

"Oh, there's a job opportunity . . ." he baited.

I jumped on the bed and turned his screen toward me. "What are you talking about?" I asked.

T. C. went on to tell me about a pastor he met at church planters' conference who had planted a socioeconomically diverse church in downtown Los Angeles and who was now looking for an associate pastor. T. C. knows how hard it is to find a good associate pastor;

in fact, an associate was one of the things that we needed the most when we were planting a church in Boston, so he had reached out to his new friend to offer prayer and support. To his surprise, the pastor had responded, "Why don't you throw your hat into the ring?"

"What do you think, babers?"

This was a legitimate question. We were in a season of grieving and discerning; we had closed the doors on our church plant, New City Covenant Church, in Boston just a few months before. It wasn't growing, in large part because we couldn't move into the neighborhood where the church was located. Planting a church, in and of itself, is hard work. But doing it in the urban core, where mistrust is high and the needs are great, is very hard unless you have buy-in from folks in the neighborhood. Since we lived in Cambridge, a city across the river and a solid twenty minutes from our target area, the obstacle was insurmountable. After a year of trying, we decided to release our launch team, made up of thirty people who had driven into the community just as we had, and put church planting on pause. The loss of that dream broke my heart. I worried I wasn't effective or doing enough for God because the plant had failed.

"I think . . ." I started, as I pulled the laptop onto my lap and looked over the job description. I flipped to the website and had a startling revelation.

"Wait! Is the church called New City too?"

T. C. nodded excitedly. "Yeah, it is."

"Well, I guess you should apply, and let's see what happens. If God's opening a door, we'll walk through it and just keep taking the next step until he says stop."

* * *

T. C. started the application process, and before we knew it, we were on a plane to Los Angeles for his interview for the associate pastor position. Soon after that, he was offered the job.

As we sat down to plan our eleven-day road trip to move our family from Boston to LA, we decided that, in addition to visiting friends and family along the way, we'd use the trip to actively practice shalom. We're lucky to be connected with so many shalom seekers across the country, so we'd stop by some of their offices and homes to see what they were doing and to drop what we were calling "love bombs": care packages of donations to help them in their work.

I sent out an SOS to our friends in ministry with connections to the cities we knew we would pass through. We only had one criteria for recipients of our care packages: they needed to be everyday peacemakers for their communities, people seeking wholeness and goodness right where they lived. Our friends came through, and before we left Boston, we had five nominations.

Five love bombs full of ordinary gifts.

1. Art supplies for an urban church plant in Boston.

2. Makeup remover and feminine care products for a church hosting a Night of Beauty for the homeless women in their community in a town in New Hampshire.

3. Office supplies to a support group teaching nonviolence in a city where homicides are at an all-time high.

4. Journals, pens, socks, and toothbrushes for a grassroots, minority-led nonprofit in New Orleans that restores dignity to women struggling with addiction and HIV/AIDS.

5. An early Mother's Day care package for a pregnant foster mom in Houston, Texas.

And finally, we'd make our way to our new home in Los Angeles to begin our lives as a ministry family at a church a few blocks away from Skid Row.

Eleven days. Eight cities. Five love bombs.

When I shared our plan for a "road trip with a purpose" with a girlfriend over one last lunch at our favorite Tex-Mex restaurant, she chuckled into her burrito. "Your family is always doing great things," she said. "You're such a big thinker."

Even though I felt unsettled at the praise, I had to admit that she was right. This is what practicing shalom in our everyday lives

looks like: notice a point of brokenness in our contexts, ask God
for his dream of wholeness, then partner with terrific schemers in
whatever way we can. It felt only natural, then, for us to look at
eleven days of togetherness in the minivan on our way to a new
adventure and assume we'd help along the way.

Also, we're incredible meddlers.

In the weeks leading up to our trip, I was excited to cheer on
peacemakers as we traveled to our new home. Yet I also struggled
with feeling that our practices of peacemaking were inadequate.
After corresponding with the lovely shalom seekers with whom
we planned to visit, I felt that every care package was sorely lacking. I looked at the packaged pens, journals, feminine products,
and socks, and I thought, "What are we doing? Is this a Target
run or kingdom work?" Sometimes I forget those can be one and
the same.

"Jesus, I want to do more for them, give more to them," I
prayed. "But I'm just a stay-at-home mama with big dreams for
brokenhearted communities. What can my value-size pack of
toothbrushes really do?"

This is the paralyzing trap of scarcity we all fall into. Remember how we have to actively fight scarcity for our own wholeness
when we say "We are enough"? The same is true for when we seek
wholeness for others. The kingdom of God is abundant, and a
Shalom Sista should always remember that.

When we look at the giant, foreboding machine of injustice,
we feel small. We think that hour we spent mentoring a youth
doesn't really change his unstable home life. We wonder if the box
of clothes given to the crisis pregnancy center matters. We think,
"Surely there's more I can do than talk to a homeless man while
handing him a cold bottle of water on a hot summer's day. Surely!"

My insecurity carried me away on an undercurrent of fear. Fear
of being overwhelmed, fear of doing too much of the wrong thing,
fear of not doing the right thing, fear that I won't even know the
difference. There's so, so very much fear, y'all.

In a world of chaos, we've been told we have to change it
by founding the next great Nobel Peace Prize–worthy initiative.

We're fed a steady diet from the "change the world" buffet. Join the Peace Corps! Do mission work! March on Washington! Attend seminary! We are gluttons for activism.

There's a curious saying from Jesus that I think about whenever I consider taking on a new cause. "Well done, good and faithful servant! You have been faithful with a few things; I will put you in charge of many things" (Matthew 25:21). What are the few things in my life, right here, right now, that God trusts I will use to bring shalom? Those matter! This ordinary life is my classroom as a Shalom Sista. These resources, however small they may be, are what the Spirit uses in his pedagogy of peacemaking.

Courtney Martin, author of the book *Do It Anyway: The New Generation of Activists*, points out the power of small and few: "Small is beautiful again. We're still committed to making broken systems (education, healthcare, prison etc.) more just, but if today, right now, all we can do is make one person's day within that system more kind, fair, or dignified, we'll devote ourselves whole-heartedly to it."

For this manifesto point, we are reclaiming small, ordinary acts of peacemaking. We are embracing our role as everyday peace-makers, right where we are, with what's in our hands. We are choosing ordinary practices of peace, every day.

When we think that what we have to offer isn't enough, we need to remember a small boy with a little bit of bread and a few fish.

* * *

It was almost evening, and the disciples came to Jesus with some instructions.

"This is a remote place, and it's already getting late. Send the crowds away, so they can go to the villages and buy themselves some food."

Jesus replied, "They do not need to go away. You give them something to eat."

"We have here only five loaves of bread and two fish," they answered.

"Bring them here to me," he said. And he directed the people to sit down on the grass. Taking the five loaves and the two fish and looking up to heaven, he gave thanks and broke the loaves. Then he gave them to the disciples, and the disciples gave them to the people. They all ate and were satisfied, and the disciples picked up twelve basketfuls of broken pieces that were left over. The number of those who ate was about five thousand men, besides women and children. (Matthew 14:15-21)

Jesus looked out and saw the five-thousand-plus people following him. They were desperate for wholeness and confident that he had their healing in his hands. He turned to his disciples and asked the logical question: Where shall we buy food for them to eat? Jesus appealed to their natural thinking, the way problems have always been solved. But he also knew he was going to solve their big problems with smallness. So he waited and watched as the disciples figured out the cost and then blanched at the enormity of it all. "Two hundred denarii worth of bread is not sufficient for them," one of the disciples said (John 6:7 NASB).

Crisis. Hunger. Unrest. Inequality. All pressed in on them: the brokenness of this world was put on display in a crowd of people in need of bread and the Bread.

Until one disciple had eyes to see a small boy and his small offering. Until one disciple married this great need with his knowledge of the greatness of Jesus' love: "There is a lad here who has five loaves and two small fish."

Hours away from giving our first love bomb, I was wishing I could do more. But I had to believe Jesus would multiply that small love bomb and the four that followed it, just as he did when he sat the people down and prayed over the offering of a little boy's lunch. As he distributed the small offering, it multiplied into a greater blessing: every hungry person was satisfied, and there was food left over for days.

God performs big miracles with small hands. When God is finished, we will all be satisfied and there will be love overflowing. I may have big dreams and a small offering, but I follow a remarkably resourceful God. And maybe big problems just need big faithfulness.

Four weeks after we moved into our new apartment here in Los Angeles, I opened my mailbox and found a note from someone at the nonprofit in New Orleans. She said she loved giving my kids a tour of the facilities. And the women who came to the office for needles and supplies loved the socks. She said we encouraged her to keep at the hard work of her job. And she told us to keep on teaching our kids to love the marginalized.

When I showed the kids the letter, T. J. beamed at me and said, "I'll never forget that road trip, Mom. I'll always remember how we dropped love bombs." Then he reached out to me for a fist bump and exclaimed, "BOOM!"

✳ ✳ ✳

In addition to choosing to practice shalom with our ordinary resources, we're choosing to practice shalom for the people in our lives we see every day. Kids and spouse are a given, I hope. But outside of our family, whom do we see on a daily basis?

In your everyday life, whom can you practice shalom for right now, Sista? What interaction seems so ordinary that you might easily overlook it, just as the disciples nearly overlooked the small boy's lunch?

Years ago on a date night, I realized how much I disliked the way I treated people in the service industry. Our server was a sweet but frazzled girl with thick glasses and a bright smile. She greeted us, gave us the specials, brought our order, and then . . . disappeared. I mean, I looked all around our section and she was nowhere to be found. I noticed that diners at several of her tables were grumbling, so I started to grumble as well. I complained to my husband about the server letting my glass of water remain half empty for most of my meal. I whined about how she never came back to check on us.

I was entitled and efficient, out in the world spending my money, expecting to always get my way. For context, Sistas, I am the daughter of a hard-nosed, no-compromise store manager. I knew the standards my mom had for her employees, and I was expecting nothing less in my own customer experience. Unfortunately, those high standards robbed the humanity from my shopping, and I lost my conviction for kindness toward those who served me. Too often I relied on impersonal metrics and surveys to determine how I'd treat the employees. I read Yelp reviews and marked the angry, snarky ones as "helpful" because, you know, the customer is always right. Right?

That night at the restaurant, T. C. was talking about his plans after seminary when I interrupted him. "Oh my goodness, can you believe our server hasn't checked on us?" I exclaimed. "Where is she?! I think we should give her a 10 percent tip instead of 20 percent." (Remember, y'all: imperfect peacemaker.)

T. C.'s eyes widened. "Babers, first off . . . *rude!* I was talking! Secondly, did you just hear yourself?"

This is why it's good to marry your best friend. He can tell you about yourself, know it landed, and then go on to butter his bread.

I stopped short. Had I just considered docking the server's tip for letting me go a few minutes without fresh water? Suddenly, I realized that I hated the consumer I was becoming. I was trying to live a life of intention in almost every part of my life . . . except, apparently, in the places where I spent my money. I had stopped caring about the servers, the cashiers, and the store reps.

That weekend I sat with Jesus and the interaction. You see, I had divorced my practices of peace from my everyday life. At this point, I was volunteering at a crisis pregnancy center and sponsoring a child in Ethiopia. If you had asked me whether I was a good person, I would have said yes. But I was not faithful enough to spread goodness and wholeness in my everyday life. I was reminded of a warning from the apostle Paul: "If I give all my possessions to feed the poor, and if I surrender my body to be burned, but do not have love, it profits me nothing" (1 Corinthians 13:3 NASB).

Love was nowhere to be seen in the way I treated people who served me every day: the barista, the bank teller, the mail carrier, our landlord.

So I decided to make a change. In my journal, I wrote,

When I am out and about, I will . . .

1. See the person behind the counter and remember one thing about them. The way they smile, their interesting tattoos, the way they part their hair. Anything that humanizes them.

2. On the phone, listen for their name, say their name back to them before jumping in to my need.

3. At the end of the call or transaction, say "Thank you" and mention one thing I loved about what they did.

I gave myself forty days to practice what I started to call "customer service shalom." I paid attention to the people in the service industry, letting Mother Teresa's words—"If we have no peace, it is because we have forgotten that we belong to each other." — mean more to me than a pretty phrase to hang on my kitchen wall. For those forty days, I treated every person in customer service as if they belonged to me and I belonged to them. And soon, we did.

Now my barista, cashier, bank teller, and hair dresser are no longer a means to an end but my allies in this life. Their hard work and attention keep me going. I pay attention to them, and I let them know that I see them.

This looks like telling Amy, my barista, that the little bear she created in my latte really made my day. It looks like letting Marge, my cashier, know that I appreciated how quickly she came to help me at the self-check even though she had two customers waiting for bags and one with a malfunctioning scale.

"Customer service shalom" has taught me how to resist the temptation of consumerism to reduce those relationships to transactions. It's one of my many practices of everyday peacemaking.

Oftentimes the people working in our banks, coffee shops, and restaurants are making minimum wage. They're barely able to make ends meet. When I come in and treat them as a means to an end, I add insult to injury. No one wakes up and wants to be treated poorly when they get to work. Their job does not strip them of their intrinsic value and worth. So I'm choosing to be a mindful consumer—mindful of the people behind the counter, mindful of my gratitude for them, and mindful of the way I communicate that worth to them.

As you go out into the world to pick up a gallon of milk or upgrade your phone, I hope you'll join me in honoring the people on the other side of the counter. Say their names and offer a sincere thank you for all that they do. I hope you'll look at the small offerings you have—the ice-cold water bottle for the homeless man on a hot day, the hour of coffee with a struggling mom, the ride to the airport for the grieving student—and know that you are changing the very fabric of the world for that person. You are binding up brokenness by your wholehearted presence.

* * *

There are so many annoyingly visionary wave-makers who start massive nonprofits that change people's lives and build community gardens that transform urban spaces. But there are many more of us: mamas in the middle, singles in the center, women with big hearts and not much money.

We're tempted to feel small, so we think small. We scarcely think of the needy because we feel impotent to help. We buy into the lie that big problems require big solutions. In her book *Every Little Thing*, Deidra Riggs writes, "Most of us will make a difference in this world, but not because of some grand or large-scale initiative. No, most of us will change our corner of the world and make an impact that stands the test of time through the small and seemingly insignificant (to us) interactions and decisions and conversations of our average days."

Maybe the machine of injustice in our cities, in our country, and in our world needs to meet the foreboding image of a woman as she takes out of her pocket whatever resource she has, loads it up in her slingshot, and hurls it right into the spinning cogs.

Practice everyday peacemaking, Sista. It'll add wholeness, and sweetness, and a new purpose to your everyday life. At the very least, it'll keep you from complaining about half-empty water glasses, which is always a good thing.

-14-

LEMONADE: WE WILL SHOW UP, SAY SOMETHING, AND BE STILL

True resistance begins with people confronting pain . . . and wanting to do something to change it.
—bell hooks

We were rushing to the car on a rainy Friday afternoon when my son pulled me under a concrete awning outside our building. "Mom, something happened at school today," he said.

Typically, when any of my kids start a sentence like this, I brace myself for run-of-the-mill school mishaps: a detention for forgotten homework, a tardy for hanging out in the hallway between classes, or a report of a really gross school lunch. I did not expect to receive the most troubling school news I'd ever heard from my kids.

"I don't want to say it in front of the rest of the family. Can we go back inside for a second?" he asked. I gave my keys to the other two and told them they could turn the radio on. We were on our way to make signs for the Special Olympics the next day, so I told them to think about what they wanted to create. "Come up with some fun ideas, guys. Ty and I will be right back."

Once inside, Tyson fidgeted with the sleeve of his raincoat and told me about a basketball game during gym class. His group of friends liked to rib on each other, but someone took it a bit too far. A tussle started on the court, and someone yelled an expletive.

"It wasn't me, Mom! I promise, I didn't cuss. But the coach heard us and ran over. Then he . . ."

Tyson's voice trailed off and he looked away. His chest heaved and his Adam's apple moved with unshed tears. "Then he . . . Mom, he's always yelling at us, especially me."

He stopped abruptly. "You know what, forget it!" he said, and tried to walk past me, reaching for the front door.

"Tyson, wait!" I grabbed his shoulders and forced him back. When his eyes met mine, the tears were already flowing.

"Tyson, what happened?"

"The coach called me the n-word today, Mom," he whispered.

He paused. I could hardly process what he just said.

"I've never been called the n-word, especially by a white man," Tyson said. "I . . . just . . . I just didn't think that still happens."

I stumbled back to a couch and Tyson followed me. I sat there, stunned, for who knows how long. I knew we couldn't sit for much longer or the younger two would grow curious. Tyson could tell the wheels in my mind were turning, because he asked, "What are you going to do?"

Honestly, I didn't know. Like my son, I didn't think that still happened. At least not in progressive Southern California.

But it did, and I had to protect my son. I flipped into Olivia Pope crisis management mode and made a mental to-do list: Find out the name of the principal's direct supervisor. In negotiations, it's always good to have the name of the boss. Research local schools' diversity and sensitivity training. Spiritually, I knew I had to have a serious come-to-Jesus before attempting to talk to that coach.

Before I could get to any of it—the meeting with the school, the chat with Jesus, the confronting of racism in the twenty-first century—I needed to care for Tyson. I needed to tend to my boy whose identity was shaken. The history of hate and brutality of that word now hovered above him, and I feared it would rob him of his worth.

I put my arm around him and squeezed his shoulder, "Don't worry, Tyson. I'll take care of it. Go wait in the car for a sec. I need to let Virginia know we'll be running late."

He nodded, wiped at his eyes and asked, "Are you going to tell anyone?"

I thought for a moment and nodded, "If it's ok. I'm kinda in new territory here, kid. Do you mind if I only tell my closest friends . . . and dad of course."

With a wry chuckle and a nod he said, "It's ok, Mom." Then he leaned down to kiss my cheek before running out into the rain.

When he was out of sight, I pulled out my phone to text my friend Virginia, who was helping us make signs. "We're going to be a little late. Tyson was called the n-word today and we had to talk about it," I texted. "We're still coming over to make signs, but I don't know what to do."

Then I put my head in my hands and wept.

＊ ＊ ＊

I'm not a big fan of talking about race. When something racially charged happens, I try to deflect. I really do. I'm in an interracial marriage, and I don't want to always attribute everything to racism. I'm madly in love with a white man. My children are as white as they are black. I cannot let racism be the first thing I think of when something terrible happens to a black person.

But how else could I make sense of what had just happened to my son? How else can I explain a black man being pummeled at a political rally, the candidate encouraging those who were hitting him, and even offering to pay legal fees? How else can I explain a young black teacher dying, on camera, when a police officer shot him on a routine traffic stop? The fierceness of my love for my kids and my confusion about racism in the world meet every single time a racially charged occurrence enters my newsfeed. Y'all, I don't know how else to interpret the hostility that comes up whenever we try to have an honest conversation about race, other than that it's incredibly hard to raise confident, loving, hopeful black children these days. "Black people love their children with a kind of obsession," writes Ta-Nehisi Coates. "You are all we have, and you come to us endangered."

I understand that for many white believers, there's a fair amount of anxiety around race these days—so much so, in fact, that we avoid having conversations about race in an effort to "keep the peace." But is this the way of Jesus?

Jesus wept in solidarity with his friends who were grieving. A Shalom Sista is a woman who looks for these moments and stands with the suffering. Whether or not she agrees with them. Whether or not she understands. She stands in solidarity.

She says, "I will show up, say something, be still."

Show up.

When racism hits a family, it doesn't just affect them; it affects everyone around them. There is a tsunami of confusion that threatens to overtake us all when we realize that racism still exists—even in 2016, even in suburban LA, even toward a biracial child.

As I pulled myself together to go out to my waiting children, my phone chimed with a new message from Virginia. "I'm here for you, friend. Whatever you need." Because my son gave me permission, I started texting and posting to Facebook to ask for help. And guess what? Shalom Sistas showed up like bosses.

During the next several days, I was surprised by the different kinds of support I received from my friends. Some friends showed up: they used their arms to hug me and their feet to prayer-walk with me just so I could vent.

Say something.

Some friends said something. When they didn't know what to do, these friends shared words of encouragement and support. They sent kind emails and shared their expertise to help me advocate for my son. They texted quirky emoticons and prayers.

Be still.

Some friends came over and just sat with me while I cried. I didn't have to rehash my story or worry about hosting them. We just sat and let the Holy Spirit heal me.

I'm grateful, because I couldn't manage all the moving parts of this broken machine by myself. I needed my people.

✳   ✳   ✳

It was amid this gratitude for community that Beyoncé's *Lemonade* album dropped.

Beyoncé's album was a prophetic narrative of the stages of grief in song and poetry, bass drops and steel drums, f-bombs and freedom calls. Every song spoke to my sadness, yet every song reminded me of my Sistas who carried me through.

Sweet Sistas, I want you to know that you don't have to give in to the feeling of inadequacy. The color of your skin does not preclude you from your specific practice of shalom in the face of racism or other injustice. The best way you can serve a mom like me when she processes this pain in her family is to just be yourself.

You can show up. Say something. Be still.

To show you that the unique way God made you is invaluable to moving the dial forward, I want to offer you some *Lemonade*-inspired guidance through my favorite tracks on Beyoncé's album.

When injustice strikes at the hearts and bodies of your friends, what kind of Shalom Sista are you?

Sista Shiva. If the first thing you thought when you read what happened to my son was "I'm so sorry this happened to you!" then you're probably a Sista Shiva. Just like the Jewish comforters who participate in the practice of sitting shiva—sitting with the

grieving for seven days with no agenda and no frills—your practice of shalom is the ministry of presence.

You're great at making space for your sister to express all her
pain. Your strength is in your kind words and faithful arms. A
fantastic hugger, you carry a purse overflowing with tissues. Your
superpower is comfort in the face of loss. With a flexible disposition, you're completely okay with sitting with sadness and letting
your friend direct on how you can help her. You're patient and
secure. You don't feel that you have to have the answers.

So when you do show up, bring a pitcher of lemonade and
add a bit of lavender honey (find a recipe on page 234), because
lavender is known for its calming properties and its flavor is best
when it is steeped overnight. I think your jam is Beyoncé's "Pray
You Catch Me." The dissonance of the beginning and the lyrics of
confusion and betrayal reflected my sadness after the news. The
quiet spaces between phrases remind me of sitting quietly with my
own Sista Shivas.

Sista Shock and Awe. If the first thing you thought when you
read what happened to my son was "Oh heck no!" then you're
probably a Sista Shock and Awe.

These Sistas made space for my anger in a way that put to
rest my fears of being labeled an "angry black woman" or "mama
bear." Sometimes when I get angry about racism, I worry that I'm
just overly sensitive. After the coach called my son the n-word, I
too often thought that maybe I was making too big a deal about
it. But the Sistas Shock and Awe in my life were not having any
of that. They're not afraid of anger. If you're a Sista Shock and
Awe, your strength is your courage. Your mission is to protect the
weak. You practice shalom by giving your friends a safe space to
be angry.

Sistas Shock and Awe are the women who'll listen as a friend
runs down a bullet point list of offenses, then give clear ideas on
how to resist the injustice. In our case, they showed up in the
school office the Monday after the racial slur was hurled at my
son to make sure everyone in the administration knew there was a
community of people who would not stand for this. Sistas Shock

and Awe know that when Jesus flipped over the tables, he did so to disrupt a system that violated the poor and oppressed.

Beyoncé's destruction of cars and fire hydrants in the music video for your anthem, "Hold Up," speaks to your anger at racism in America.

But anger balances on a knife-edge, doesn't it? It can quickly become sin. So, Sista Shock and Awe, while I think "Hold Up" is so your spicy jam, when you visit your Sista in need and crank up those first few bars of steel drums to begin your war dance, let's leave the bat in the storage closet, m'kay? Your challenge will be to remember that we wrestle not with flesh and blood but against the spiritual forces of evil in the heavenly realms.

Sista Safekeeper. If the first thing you thought when you read what happen to my son was "What can I do for you?" then you're probably a Sista Safekeeper.

When something as massive as racism hits a family, it's very easy to think that the philosophical and political efforts to fight it are more important than everything else. I can throw myself into the work of justice—the meetings, the phone calls, the writing of op-eds and letters to officials—and everything else falls by the wayside. For several days, we didn't cook or clean, and I only showered once. I was so focused on figuring out what to do to fix the school and help my son. Before I knew it, we spiraled downward as a family—no one ate a healthy meal, no one slept, no one laughed. All our conversations were consumed by this offense.

Sista Safekeepers remind those of us in the trenches to take care of ourselves. When we can't do it for ourselves, they show up with a casserole in hand and gentle encouragement to go take a nap. Sista Safekeepers are the subversive and irreverent voices for self-care that make a mom like me stop spinning out and begin to listen to my own needs. During this crisis, they gave me permission to unapologetically ask for what I needed from my family and, eventually, from the school. If you're a Sista Safekeeper, when you see a family in crisis, your first instinct is to surround them with practical help.

These are the Sistas who pushed me out of the house to go to small group because they knew I needed to be there. When I mentioned that my son was feeling unsafe at school after the incident, a whole community of Sista Safekeepers spent the morning texting my son, making him laugh with silly memes and jokes. He came home from school grateful for encouraging words that helped him to keep his head up.

So, Sista Safekeeper, it's no surprise that your jam is Beyoncé's "Sorry"—it's an anthem of self-care and claiming your worth in the midst of trauma. You might be tempted to be a little pushy, because you can perceive something as a need and then relentlessly push your Sista to do it. Be careful; your good intentions could accidentally offend. Your challenge will be to follow the lead of your Sista—she'll get there eventually.

Sista Shackle-Breaker. If the first thing you thought when you read what happened to my son was "This is their chance to help change a broken system," then you're probably a Sista Shackle-Breaker.

These are the women in my life who saw the threads of my story in two directions: reaching back to continue the justice work of the past, and stretching forward to create a new future. Because they are such visionaries, they reminded me that I'm part of God's larger story of shalom. They're "holy hype girls" who kept me on mission in the face of my own self-doubt.

So many times during this crisis, I asked, "Can I really take on the school and administrators? Is this even worth it?" The Sista Shackle-Breakers' answer to me was a "Yes, girl! Yes!" Because of their support, I didn't quit.

My Sista Shackle-Breakers offered to stage a protest to make sure no other brown child on that campus would suffer as my son had. They posted to social media about what happened and invited me over to talk about next steps. If you're a Sista Shackle-Breaker, you get excited about learning policies and befriending decision makers. You practice shalom by mobilizing us to bring about justice, but your primary challenge is to work in community for that change.

You have the tendency to be impatient—you see what needs to be done and you want to move. Now. But remember, Sista: this is a community movement toward wholeness. You have to learn to walk in step with the women you don't quite get—the ones who have to sit in their pain for a bit longer than you're comfortable. I know, dear one; sometimes this feels like inactivity. But under the stillness of the surface, something profound is happening. God is doing the deeper work of binding our hearts together so that when we move against hatred, we're a unified force of love. Since you're so passionate about long-term flourishing, your jam can be no other than Beyoncé's "Freedom." (I love this song too, but I do think Beyoncé got something wrong. We can't break these chains all by ourselves; we need each other.)

These are the four types of friends who buoyed me when I felt as if I were drowning during the month after the coach called my son the n-word. I needed them all.

* * *

White women sometimes ask me a question in response to something I've written on racism, privilege, or diversity. "I really want to talk about this, but I don't think I have the right to," they'll say. "I mean . . . I'm white."

To which I say: You actually need to talk about race *because* you're white. Because you haven't had to think about it, you need to think about it now. You need to hear my story as a black woman in America so you can share it with your white friends.

The truth is, your voice matters, and it has power. As a white believer, your acknowledgment of my experience brings a much-needed validation to the racism I dealt with as a young, insecure black girl in a predominately white community. If I know you care enough to listen, then I know I can trust you and can hear the best of your words. Speak up and speak life! Your voice can reverberate across the wounded places of my heart. The echoes of your acceptance have the power to heal deep, deep offenses.

Because you are white, you need to reject the allure of avoiding the topic altogether to talk instead about sexy husbands, deep calls from Jesus, oppressed women in other countries, patriarchy in the Western church, or tasty recipes. I don't have that luxury. I engage with the world as a black woman. I live with the reality that if you and I had known each other during the Jim Crow era, my son could have been tortured and murdered for telling your daughter she's beautiful. If you ignore this, then I'm sorry, honey, but I think your privilege is showing.

So even though you are white, please speak up! Don't deflect by saying we should care about more important topics. That invalidates the offense. Please say to your African American friends that you want to understand their frustration. Maybe you can't relate, and that's okay. But for the love of God, please start the conversation!

I need to see that. I think that in these critical times, you can show up, say something, and be still.

* * *

Take a few deep, cleansing breaths with me, Sista. We did it. We talked about race and no one spontaneously combusted. I've been in many a conversation about race, and in some cases, the participants probably wished they could have combusted just to avoid the pain and awkwardness. There's a strong chance you read about my Sistas Shiva, Safekeeper, Shock and Awe, and Shackle-Breaker and didn't see yourself in any of them. Maybe all of this is new to you. Maybe you're not sure you'd know what to do, because this conversation scares you.

It's okay. I'm black, and this conversation scares me to the core—so much so that the night before I went to talk to the coach who called my son the n-word, I couldn't sleep. I lay there in bed thinking about all the responses I had for him. Some were great zingers. Some were tearful pleas for him to apologize to our son. Some were indignant responses. And I'll admit it: some were threats. Honestly, I had no idea what to do.

But I resolved that when racism threatened to paralyze me and rob me of my chance to practice shalom, I would resist. I would show up. I would say something. And I would be still. For my son.

Show up.

My husband; our friend Delonte, a black man who did advocacy work in Washington, D.C.; and I met with the school administrators. We were on time. We were kind. We shook hands with everyone—even the offending teacher. After the obligatory reading of the report, the principal turned it over to us and asked, "Is there anything you'd like to say?"

Say something.

With a lump in my throat and a cocktail of anger, hurt, and sadness in my belly, I said yes. I told the officials how disappointed I was, how I understood that there might have been a miscommunication but such language is never appropriate. I revealed that this experience made our family, who was still so new to the community, feel extremely unsafe. I offered the benefit of doubt and asked, "How can we partner together so this never happens again?"

Be still.

That evening, when Tyson came home, I poured him a glass of milk and we sat at the table with our favorite snack: Oreo cookies. I told him about the meeting. The school had offered a diplomatic apology—the kind where they could not deny or confirm that something happened but said they would do everything in their power to prevent it in the future. It sure wasn't what we had hoped for. But it was a start. We're still dealing with this issue on my son's campus; it's a long road toward racial justice.

With tears in his eyes, Tyson cleared his throat and said, "I'm not sure I want to go back there. I'm so angry."

"Well, son," I said, quieting my anxiety about what our other options for schooling might be. "I'm here for you, and I'll support you, no matter what."

He nodded, and dunked his cookie (super gross). I twisted mine apart so that I could eat it deconstructed (like a refined human being). We sat in silence.

I'm not sure what's next for us. To be honest, sometimes it feels as though I'm just waiting for our next brush with racism. I am raising two brown boys in America, y'all.

But I'll be okay. I've got my Sista Shiva to hold me when I cry. I've got my Sista Shock and Awe to help me process my anger in a safe space. My Sista Safekeeper makes sure I value myself and my needs before caring for others. And my Sista Shackle-Breaker keeps me on mission.

With these Sistas, when life gives our black family lemons, we will for sure make lemonade. And dance it out in my living room to Beyoncé. Always.

-15-

KINGDOM STRONG: WE WILL BE PEACEMAKERS, NOT PEACEKEEPERS

Even those who have committed great violence can have the image of God come to life again within them as they hear the whisper of love. May the whisper of love grow louder than the thunder of violence. May we love loudly.
—Shane Claiborne

If you were to ask me, Sista, why they did it, I would have no good explanation why they consistently treated me with such contempt and neglect! All I'd ever done was love them, and care for them, and clothe them, and wipe their little bums. On top of all that, I'd spent hours crafting meal plans and grocery lists and ambling in the store aisles looking for their favorite types of seaweed. And yet they had no gratitude. Every single night I would go to my pantry or refrigerator, and I'd find it—evidence of their carelessness. Empty boxes. Empty gallons of milk with a few drops in the bottom. Empty egg cartons. Empty cookie sleeves. Why couldn't they just throw them away?

The trash and the recycling bin were mere steps away, Sistas. You grab a snack, you realize you took the last one, and you throw the carton away. Simple.

I'd been mothering these insatiable, grazing children for years, and every day it was the same. You could find me wondering (read: ranting) about this around nine thirty after we'd put the kids to bed and I was craving a little snack. Maybe a few cubes of cheese and the good crackers (saltines have no place in my evening snacking). Or a slice of raisin bread and pat of butter. Maybe I'd make some chai with a splash of milk.

I'd go to the kitchen and find two things. One: they'd eaten it all. Two: they'd left the packaging. Do you know how frustrating it is to think you've got raisin bread, only to find the cinnamon-covered crumbs? This could not be borne, Sistas. I had to act.

So, several years ago I devised a plan that I was *this* close to enacting.

I was going to quietly collect the packaging. When they left the milk jug with only a few teaspoons of milk, I wouldn't rant. No more raving. No more questioning. Just collecting. I'd put the items in black trash bags and keep them in the back of my closet. When the children asked about the bags, I'd tell them I was planning a very special gift for them. Finally, when those bags were bursting, with sharp corners of cracker boxes poking from the sides, I'd enlist T. C.'s help.

One night, while the children were sleeping peacefully, tummies full of good crackers and warm milk, T. C. and I would stand over their beds on chairs—T. C. with the boys in their room, me with the girl. And upon my count we would empty those bags on their heads, chanting, "reduce, reuse, recycle . . . retribution!"

We would dump and chant as those boxes' edges jabbed their little elbows and curdled milk plopped in their hair.

And then we'd make the kids clean it up all up and throw the trash away outside. Maybe my kids would remember to use the trash can and recycling bin after that. (Again, Sistas: I'm not your typical peacemaker.)

One night I was thinking through the logistics of this plan, feeling equal parts gleeful and vengeful, while standing in line at the grocery store in Cambridge. Then I saw a headline that put a damper on my plan. It was an issue of *People* magazine about three women, all of whom had lost limbs in a terrorist attack. The headline read "Boston Strong: 7 Weeks Later."

Standing in line, and then waiting as the sales clerk rang up my gallon of milk and seaweed for the kids, I read the survivors' stories. I was immediately taken back to the night we found out that the Boston bombers were likely hiding in our neighborhood.

It was the night I had to reckon with my love for violence, revenge, and my desire to use both to keep the peace. That night I had to decide whether I wanted to be a peacemaker or a peace-keeper. Suddenly, there in the checkout line, my little plan for vengeance didn't seem so brilliant after all.

* * *

The Boston Marathon is an annual tradition attracting over half a million people. Since I don't run, I had no idea how big a deal it was until we moved to Boston. It seemed as if everyone I knew there was either running in the marathon or going down to the finish line on Newbury Street to cheer on their loved ones.

You know the story: On April 15, 2013, two Chechen-American brothers, Dzhokhar Tsarnaev and Tamerlan Tsarnaev, dropped a backpack with a bomb at the finish line, killing three and injuring hundreds. Three days later, after the FBI released their pictures, the brothers killed an MIT security guard, kidnapped a man, and then engaged in a shoot-out.

Two miles from our home.

When we got the news that the Boston Marathon bombers were at large in our neighborhood, I had to think about what I would do if they came to our back door. Our house was within the "lockdown" radius, and officers warned us that the brothers were armed and dangerous.

With newscasts outlining the brother's attack and their subsequent crime spree, I was forced to ask: If one those boys came to my porch intending to hurt us, what would I do? Would I use violence to protect my family, or would I listen to Jesus and "put away my sword"? Would I be a *peacekeeper*, who uses force to keep the peace for myself and my family, or a *peacemaker*, who rejects violence of all kinds?

By now you know I'm a mama who loves her babies something fierce—even though they leave empty food packages in my pantry. And Lord help you if you hurt them. Case in point: I once gave the evil eye to a ten-year-old kid who pushed my six-year-old son around on the playground. I just stared that baby down, waiting for his mom to say something to me. The whole time I told myself, "If he doesn't stop messing with my boy or if she doesn't say something soon, it's about to get really real by the merry-go-round."

After the marathon bombing, I sat and watched the evening news with my husband. The brothers had entered our neighborhood just hours before. Our kids were already in bed, but after watching the news, I couldn't sleep. I was vacillating between readying for battle and conscientiously objecting.

T. C. went to bed. He was confident of our safety. I wasn't. I had just had donuts with my kids at the very Dunkin' Donuts where the newscasters were reporting from. We knew that street where the first gunfight had taken place. We passed it on the way to the library.

The manhunt was real, and I had three sleeping children who needed someone to keep vigil. So I stayed up.

And like Jacob wrestling with an angel, I wrestled with Jesus.

✻ ✻ ✻

Praying and pacing, at one point I began to make plans. Okay. If he bangs on the door, we just won't open it. But the kids will probably wake up, so I'll have to hide them someplace while T. C. and I deal with him. He could shoot open the door or window and force his way in, though. What should I grab to protect the kids? Oh! Tyson has a bat in the coat closet.

But then I knew I'd be tempted to beat the ever-living daylights out of him, which is responding violently, so . . . no. Okay, okay, so no bat. What about bug spray? That's right. When he comes to the door, he'll bang on it. I'll hide the kids. T. C. will reason with him, but if that doesn't work, I'll spray him down good. But I knew I'd just escalate the conflict with a person who had a gun. That seemed neither Christlike nor smart.

Fine! So no bat, no bug spray. What else could I use?

Then, right in the middle of my manic musings, I felt convicted. I can't say I heard an actual voice, but I may as well have, given how clearly the thought occurred to me. "Why do you need *anything*? You have me, don't you?"

My soul went still and silent.

And that's the crux of it. I wanted a clear, step-by-step guide for nonviolence that would offer the peaceful solution for every possible violent action. And there isn't any. I can't accurately predict the behavior of sentient, free-will beings. The only sentient, free-will being I can control is myself. Knowing that Jesus saw nonviolence through—even to an excruciating end—I had to release my need to defend, control, and predict.

I needed to take heed of Jesus' rebuke to Peter in the garden and put away my sword.

Mother Teresa offers a gentle reminder, one that I was coming to terms with that night: "We do not need guns and bombs to bring peace, we need love and compassion." Do I love the Lord enough to resist violence? Do I have enough compassion for another human being to honor the image of God in that person? These are the questions we have to ask if we want to follow Jesus' example of nonviolence. If we want to be women who put away the sword.

The more I study the kingdom ethic of nonviolence, the more I'm learning that loving the Lord with all my strength requires that I lay down conventional strength of force so that I may love my neighbor as myself. Nonviolence requires a conscious dependence on the Holy Spirit that is rooted in our conviction that the Spirit is both real and resourceful. Nonviolence means trusting that there's enough creativity in creator God to extend to my moment of crisis. Nonviolence says that if somehow my children watch me die because I chose to heal when someone meant to harm, there will be resurrection power for their loss. My death will breathe life into their faith to love like Jesus, live like Jesus, and die like Jesus—because their mama did.

I wish I could tell you I was filled with a renewed sense of purpose at that moment. I wasn't. I still sat for hours watching the news and crying. I knew Jesus was all I needed, and yet he didn't feel like enough.

At some point in the middle of the night, I went to bed and prayed until I fell asleep, "Jesus, help me be okay with you and only you. Help me be okay. Help me be okay . . . help me be okay . . ."

I woke up with the sun streaming into my room and my children asking for Cheerios.

We "sheltered in place" that day, staying in our house as we were told to while SWAT teams, helicopters, and police officers searched for the remaining suspect. Thankfully, we were on the opposite side of their search radius, so my children were spared the trauma of determined men with readied guns invading our home.

But all day long I still prayed, "Jesus, help me be okay . . . help me be okay . . . help me be okay . . ." I have to admit: he wasn't enough, in a way. I still wanted to defend my children to the death. But that night I sat with the Bible and asked Jesus, what are the things that make for peace in a violent world? I found comfort in a surprising place. Not in a well-thought-out plan to thwart violence, but in Jesus' final hours before the cross, when his love and intention met to show us how to be true peacemakers and not just peacekeepers.

*   *   *

The last things I say to my children before they head out for school are always the most important.

"Don't forget your folder!"

"Here's your lunch box!"

"Eat the carrots first!"

"I love you!"

I say these words before they step off the security of my porch and into the vulnerability of a new day. They are my last-ditch efforts to give them everything they need to be their best selves when they're not with me.

This is probably why I paid special attention to Jesus in his last hours before his death. From the Last Supper to the cross, I knew that these were Jesus' last-ditch efforts to give his disciples, present and future, everything they needed to be their best selves when he was no longer with them.

In the garden, after his betrayal, Jesus could have kept the peace by force. He could have unleashed his loyal remnant—a ragtag band of brothers with swords—on the Roman soldiers. Instead, he rejected violence and healed a soldier after Peter lost his temper and cut off his ear. Jesus said, "'No more of this!' And he touched the man's ear and healed him" (Luke 22:51). Jesus could have ordered an attack, but he offered healing. Let's not overlook this clear example from our true Prince of Peace.

Then, standing before Pontius Pilate, Jesus could have defended himself, thus keeping political peace and appeasing Pilate. But he spoke of the kingdom of God.

> Then Pilate went back into the palace and called for Jesus to be brought to him. "Are you the King of the Jews?" he asked him.
>
> "'King' as you use the word or as the Jews use it?" Jesus asked.
>
> "Am I a Jew?" Pilate retorted. "Your own people and their chief priests brought you here. Why? What have you done?"

> Then Jesus answered, "I am not an earthly king. If I were, my
> followers would have fought when I was arrested by the Jewish
> leaders. But my Kingdom is not of the world."
>
> Pilate replied, "But you are a king then?"
>
> "Yes," Jesus said. "I was born for that purpose. And I came to
> bring truth to the world. All who love the truth are my follow-
> ers." (John 18:33-37 TLB)

Again, after hours of torture, betrayal, humiliation, and excruciating pain, Jesus could have cared about keeping his own emotional peace. He could have commanded angels to come and end
his suffering, or even just transferred a small portion of his pain to
the crowd by calling out hateful accusations to every person at the
foot of the cross. But no.

> Jesus turning to them said, "Daughters of Jerusalem, stop weep-
> ing for Me, but weep for yourselves and for your children. For
> behold, the days are coming when they will say, 'Blessed are the
> barren, and the wombs that never bore, and the breasts that
> never nursed.' Then they will begin to say to the mountains,
> 'Fall on us,' and to the hills, 'Cover us.' For if they do these
> things when the tree is green, what will happen when it is dry?"
> Two others also, who were criminals, were being led away to be
> put to death with Him. . . .
>
> One of the criminals who were hanged there was hurling abuse
> at Him, saying, "Are You not the Christ? Save Yourself and
> us!" But the other answered, and rebuking him said, "Do you
> not even fear God, since you are under the same sentence of
> condemnation? And we indeed are suffering justly, for we are
> receiving what we deserve for our deeds; but this man has done
> nothing wrong." And he was saying, "Jesus, remember me when
> You come in Your kingdom!" And He said to him, "Truly I say
> to you, today you shall be with Me in Paradise." (Luke 23:28-
> 32, 39-43 NASB)

And when he took his last breath and whispered, "It is finished,"
Jesus reconciled us to God by revealing the truest characteristic of
the Father: his self-giving love that is the bedrock of his kingdom.
N. T. Wright says it best: "The whole point of the kingdom of
God is Jesus has come to bear witness to the true truth, which

is nonviolent. When God wants to take charge of the world, he doesn't send in the tanks. He sends in the poor and the meek."

If everything Jesus said and did in those last hours had the same earnest intent I have when I send my babies off to school, then nonviolence is among the most important things he wants us to remember.

When he healed the Roman soldier in the garden of Gethsemane, Jesus taught the kingdom principle of peacemaking: when there's a clear and justifiable opportunity to hurt, choose to heal. Here's what he said:

> Put your sword back where it belongs. All who use swords are destroyed by swords. Don't you realize that I am able right now to call to my Father, and twelve companies—more, if I want them—of fighting angels would be here, battle-ready? But if I did that, how would the Scriptures come true that say this is the way it has to be? (Matthew 26:52-54 *The Message*)

Can you imagine the impact Jesus' nonviolent resistance made on that soldier's life? Can you imagine how he looked into the Savior's eyes as his ear, bloody and jagged from Peter's blade, miraculously rejoined his body? Can you imagine the love he found there? The acceptance? The forgiveness? The peace?

I can. That's why I'm compelled be a peacemaker who heals, not just a peacekeeper who defends.

After the bombings, a rallying cry arose to fight back the anxiety of the violence: "We are Boston Strong." Boston Strong showed up everywhere after the attack—on the news, at the store, in every train station and bus stop. We could not get away from this reminder that we will persist.

But "Boston Strong," while a catchy phrase, has the cadence of "Pax Romana." We will secure our peace. We will protect our own. We will strike fear in the hearts of our enemies. We will manufacture peace with force.

Sounds familiar doesn't it?

So after we sheltered in place and I committed wholeheartedly to nonviolent resistance, I decided to never buy or say "Boston Strong." Because I'm not. I am a Shalom Sista; I am Kingdom Strong.

When you reject the violence and fear of this world, you too are Kingdom Strong. You are a peacemaker, not a peacekeeper.

* * *

Being a peacemaker is a courageous calling that the world needs us to answer. We are the children of God, we have the Holy Spirit who has transformed us into new creations made of sterner stuff than to merely keep the peace. Every day we have to decide whether we'll take Jesus' challenge to live as peacemakers and not simply as peacekeepers. The difference is subtle but important.

Peacekeeping is a result of our fear. But perfect love casts out fear, so peacemaking flourishes from our love: love for God, love for people, love for the world.

Peacekeeping maintains the unjust status quo by preferring the powerful. Peacemaking flips over a few tables in the courtyards of oppression and dismantles systems that exploit the poor.

Peacekeeping does everything to secure a place at the table. Peacemaking says all are welcome at the table, then extends the table with leaves of inclusive love.

Peacekeeping worries about your own comfort. Peacemaking takes notice of the discomfort of those around you.

Peacekeeping is for districts and factions and empires. Peacemaking is the kingdom of God.

* * *

"Wake up! Look what's on HBO!" T. C. was shaking me awake. I had fallen asleep on the couch, which is a normal occurrence after ten at night.

Groggily, I sat up in our living room in Los Angeles. "What?"

"It's a documentary following the Boston bombing survivors," he said. "Remember when the bombers hid in Watertown and because we were within a two-mile radius, we had to shelter in place while the police searched for them?"

Of course I did. It was the day I had to decide whether I was going to be a peacemaker or a peacekeeper.

At the end of the documentary, there was a collection of interviews with the survivors of the Boston Marathon bombing, many of whom had lost limbs. The filmmaker asked the survivors about the recent news that Dzhokhar Tsarnaev had been sentenced to death by execution.

Almost every single one of the survivors supported the death penalty. The deaths and injuries were so great, and the devastation on our beloved city was so palpable, of course they should die. Right? Several of the survivors cited the rallying cry after the bombing—We are Boston Strong—for why the punishment was appropriate. There was no talk of love, creativity, or honoring the humanity of the perpetrator. Just revenge and bravado. I was in tears by the credits. I did not want that boy to die. I want peace for the Tsarnaev brothers and their families. I want healing and a chance for redemption for the one who still lives.

I wanted peacemakers to rise up on behalf of this teenager turned terrorist.

I think the hardest thing about being a Shalom Sista is accepting that God's dream for wholeness extends to people like the Tsarnaev brothers. This is one of those instances where two manifesto points go hand in hand: I have to tell a better story about the boys behind the Boston bombing if I want to be a peacemaker for them.

So I will choose the way of the cross that says "I'd rather die for you than kill to protect myself." Preston Sprinkle says, "The nonviolent rhythms of the cross meet the melodies of this world with dissonance." Lord, may the nonviolent rhythm of the cross meet our worlds every single day.

Now, years later, I'm almost there. I'm almost okay. Following Jesus means responding the way he responded to violence. That requires a daily putting away of my sword. It's one of the most difficult decisions of my faith, but it's one I'm committed to seeing through.

There will be more opportunities to trust in my own abilities. They won't be as sensational as car chases, gunfights, and a terrorist, but they'll still matter. They just might be as ordinary as planning vengeful lessons for kids who leave empty milk cartons in the fridge and cracker boxes on the counter. Peacekeeping looks like terrorizing my children with a midnight attack of all the empty recyclables. While peacemaking looks like patiently calling the kids in to throw their trash away, repositioning or purchasing more recycling bins, or maybe even charging an empty-box tax from their allowances. The point is not to have a clear plan, but an eager heart to choose peacemaking over peacekeeping because that's the legacy I want to leave for my children.

A legacy of stubborn love and redemptive peace.

A legacy of a mama who was troubled but took heart, because Jesus has overcome the world.

A legacy of a woman who consciously depends on the Holy Spirit, because Jesus is enough.

So I still pray, "Jesus, help me be okay with you. Only you. No matter what comes. When I want to resort to my own devices, help me remember to put my sword away. Help me heal when I want to hurt. Help me be Kingdom Strong."

We, Sistas, are peacemakers, not peacekeepers. We lead with love, not anxiety. With God's help, we put away our swords.

EPILOGUE

And so we are at the end of our time together, Sistas. If you were here in my home, I'd pack up leftover snacks and send them with you in my Tupperware—no worries on getting the containers back to me. We'd hug at my door and I'd ask a question I learned from one of my mentors, "Can I pray for you before you leave?"

This prayer before you leave, I've learned in church, is called a benediction. I used to think benedictions, and the giving of them, were something reserved for professional clergy: those with collars and MDivs.

That is, until I met Pastor Judy at family camp one summer.

As the camp pastor, she taught the adults every day while the kids went off to a Bible school program. At the end of her sessions, no matter what she preached on, Pastor Judy would say, "My friends, Jesus met us today in Scripture, but now we're tasked with taking it out into our lives. I invite you to stand with me, reach your arms out as if you are receiving a gift, and hear this benediction."

It was my favorite part of family camp that year: standing with my arms reached out, receiving a blessing to live out the truth I learned that morning.

Over lunch one day that week, I told Pastor Judy how much her benedictions meant to me. She replied, "It's really important for me to make the receiving of a benediction something my congregants embody. That way they can feel empowered to go out into the world and offer benedictions wherever they go."

This idea—that we are walking benedictions, giving blessings and pronouncing goodness wherever we go—is what it means to be a Shalom Sista.

Later, I read *An Altar in the World* by Barbara Brown Taylor, and she reminded me of Pastor Judy's encouragement.

> As someone who has been paid to pronounce blessings at weddings and funerals, at baptisms and house blessings, at soup kitchens and foxhunts—as well as at lots and lots of weekly worship services—I think it is a big mistake to perpetuate the illusion that only certain people can bless things. This kind of blessing prayer is called a benediction. It comes at the end of something, to send people on their way. All I am saying is that anyone can do this. Anyone can ask and anyone can bless, whether anyone has authorized you to do it or not. All I am saying is that the world needs you to do this, because there is a real shortage of people willing to kneel wherever they are and recognize the holiness.

And so, as we come to a close, I'd like to give you a benediction as you seek shalom (and you can find some recipes for snacks at the end of this book).

> May you, sweet Sista, celebrate all the different ways we bring shalom in our everyday lives: the ownership of our belovedness, the proclamation that we are enough, the beauty we choose to see, the ways we rest, the joy we claim, the better stories we tell, the walls we tear down in order to build bridges, the humility in our service, the ways we resist division and stand in solidarity, the peace we make, every single ordinary day.

> May you remember to breathe in the presence of our Prince of Peace. Like the disciples in the upper room after Jesus was resurrected, we stand together, preparing to go out into the world

as ambassadors of the kingdom of God. Jesus longs to breathe on us, give us the Holy Spirit, and empower us to be everyday peacemakers.

For Jesus said, blessed are the peacemakers, they will be called daughters of God

Our hearts beat to the anthem of the kingdom. The harmony of shalom thrums wildly in our veins. Peacemaking, after all, is written into our spiritual DNA.

There is nothing as effective in binding up brokenness on earth as love. Therefore, may you be a woman who loves, because you've been dearly loved.

We have been made whole, so may you be a woman who witnesses pain and waits for your chance to heal.

May you feel empowered to heal with your words; they are never weapons but rather instruments for telling better stories. Heal with your hands, Sista, which are always open and busy building bridges. Heal with your humility, which invites others and teaches them how to love better. May you have the courage to show up where there is suffering, say something redemptive, and create spaces for stillness.

I pray that you embrace all of yourself as good, very good. Be creative and quirky. Don't take yourself too seriously. Dance it out in your living room. Look for joy triggers. Subvert despair with your song of hope.

With eyes that have caught the beauty of the kingdom, I bless you to look around and say, "I will see the beauty," and then call it out, Sista. Your voice is needed.

May you choose the peace of the kingdom over fear, striving, and violence—in both word and deed.

Because when we listen to fear, it paralyzes us. When we listen to striving, it humiliates us. When we listen to violence, it dehumanizes us.

So, let us reject these lies and listen to the Truth.

Let us, be bright spots of Light where there is darkness.

Let us, run, skip, jump, twirl, and dance all the way home, for we are practitioners of a subversive joy.

Let us remember that we belong to each other.

For Sista, I belong to you and you belong to me, and we are Beloved, we are Enough, we are Beautiful.

We are Shalom Sistas.

May you find your place in our revolution for peace.

Amen.

Shalom Steps

On my podcast and website, I like to give Shalom Steps: practical next steps to take what we've learned about peacemaking and apply it to our lives. I once read that wedding gown designer Vera Wang designs gowns for brides with three considerations: does it fit her, is it beautiful, and can she dance in it? Well, Sistas, these Shalom Steps are here to help you. Take the ones that fit your personality, embrace the beauty of shalom found in each one, and dance. I can't wait to see all the ways you live our God's radical peace right where you are. Will you share them with me online with the hashtag #ShalomSista?

WE ARE INVITED

- **Practice imaginative prayer.** Imaginative prayer is shared experience with Jesus that is based on stories of Jesus from the Gospels and that draws on our use of empathy and visualization. Choose your favorite story and imagine yourself as the person receiving love and care from the Lord.
- **Seek out a spiritual director.** A spiritual director's goal is sit with you and help you hear from God. They're trained to do just that.

- Correct others when they paint a picture of God that doesn't look like Jesus. This can be difficult, but don't be afraid to try.
- **Dance!** You can start with the Shalom Sistas' playlist online. Find it on my website, Shalominthecity.com.

WE ARE BELOVED

- **Read *Life of the Beloved* by Henri Nouwen.** This book is on my yearly "to read" list. In a world that's always asking us to prove it, we need a regular dose of wisdom and recentering of our identity in Christ. Nouwen's book is my favorite.
- **Tell yourself you are beloved.** Every morning for one month, before you do anything else, tell yourself you are beloved. This can help you break the connection between value and output.
- **Ask for help.** If you feel unstable emotionally, or if things don't feel right, don't be afraid to ask for help. Seek out therapy, let your community know, call a suicide prevention hotline. Don't suffer alone, my Sista.
- **Tell yourself that others are beloved.** When you go through your day, practice telling yourself that every person you meet is a beloved person. How does this change the way you think about him or her? Do you sense compassion growing for strangers by knowing you both are beloved by God?

WE ARE ENOUGH

- **Identify one area where you may feel like an imposter.** Where do you feel you don't belong or that you're not "good enough"? Reject the shame that comes from imposterism.
- **Practice *lectio divina*.** *Lectio divina* is a traditional Benedictine practice of Scripture-reading, meditation, and prayer. Read a passage three times, stopping after each time through to consider what stands out to you and what the Spirit is saying to you. Try *lectio divina* with Jesus' time in the wilderness (Matthew 4). Ask the Lord to show you where you feel inadequate. Ask him to nourish your soul with his words.

- **Identify a hype song and power pose to go with it.** My favorite is "Girl on Fire" by Alicia Keys. Stand like Superman or in a spread-eagle pose for the duration of the song.
- **Reach out to other "imposters."** Make a list of people you know who have struggled with feelings of imposterism, inadequacy, or perfectionism. Reach out to them and tell them three things you love about them. Let them know you are happy they are in your life.

We Will See the Beauty

- **Reflect on definitions of beauty.** Think about standards of beauty you've grown up with or accepted. What is considered unacceptable or undesirable?
- **Practice seeing beauty in "unlovely" bodies.** Make a Pinterest board of people who embody the "wrong" kind of body. Invite the Holy Spirit to guide you as you look through the pictures and note the beauty in the image. It's okay to start with the scenery or the model's outfit. Make it a practice to gaze on those images until you begin to see the beauty in the person herself.
- **Invite a friend to go on a beauty walk.** Choose a scenic location: a garden, a park, a museum, the beach, or another place that stirs your soul. Your one mission: to honestly share your body-shame stories, struggles, or both, and then encourage each other to call out three beautiful things about your bodies, right then, as they are. At the end of this time, say: "My body is wholly good."
- **Surround yourself with words of encouragement.** Find words and images like my friend's "You are beautiful" decals. Etsy has some gorgeous printables too.

We Will Rest

- **Observe the Sabbath.** Decide to observe the Sabbath by blocking out ten hours in your week to rest. Make a list of things you want to do in those ten hours a week. Now, circle the items on that list that will take five hours or fewer to do. Plan to do one of them a week for the next month.

- **Help someone else observe the Sabbath.** With the remaining time, find out how you can offer yourself as an agent of mercy and goodness for someone in your community. An easy place to start is by asking your kids' teachers or your pastors if they notice anyone who feels overwhelmed or overworked. Reach out and offer specific one-time help. It'll be awkward, but you can do it, I promise! Here's your script:

> Hey there, [Awesome Person Whose Kid Is in My Kid's Class]. I was wondering if maybe I could help you out a bit by taking your daughter out for ice cream with mine after school next Tuesday. Then you can take your time getting home from work and maybe stop off and have a latte—on me. Life is overwhelming for all of us sometimes; I've been there, and I just want to help.

WE WILL CHOOSE SUBVERSIVE JOY

- **Make two lists: one of pain triggers, another of joy triggers.** Like the psalmist, pray over every item on the pain list and rejoice over the items on the joy list. This is not insensitive; we're taking a cue from our Lord, "who for the joy set before Him endured the cross, despising the shame, and has sat down at the right hand of the throne of God" (Hebrews 12:2 NASB). We hold the pain of the world in tension with the joy of the kingdom.
- **Commit Nehemiah 8:10 to memory:** "Go and enjoy choice food and sweet drinks, and send some to those who have nothing prepared. This day is holy to our Lord. Do not grieve, for the joy of the Lord is your strength."
- **Place joy triggers in your home.** Orange and yellow promote optimism. Consider buying a vase in one of those colors and keep it full of fresh flowers. (But if baby poop green makes your heart sing, then go for it, Sista.)
- **Offer to throw an office party for your favorite local non-profit or church.** The staff of these organizations are always

looking deeply into the hurt of the world, so give them a chance to access joy.

WE WILL TELL BETTER STORIES

- **Imagine a backstory for your "enemies."** Think about whom you would consider your enemies. Usually, it's the people just beyond your empathy. Create a backstory for them. What do you think caused them to be so angry/violent/hateful/hurtful/grubby? You don't have to know the details to create a story; you just need a holy imagination and desire to have compassion for them.
- **Think of this backstory. Often.** Decide that for the next week, whenever you think of this person or people, you will tell their backstory to yourself. Every time you tell the backstory, pay attention to the compassion that grows in your heart. Cultivate that.
- **Share your commitment.** Tell a trusted friend about your commitment to love your enemy. Ask the friend to pray for you.

WE WILL SERVE BEFORE WE SPEAK

- **Think about your deep gladness.** Reread Frederick Buechner's thoughts on calling on page 159. Where is your deep gladness? What makes you coo and light up?
- **Think about the world's deep hunger.** What problems in the world move your soul? Consider again your answers to the previous step, and write a list of all the different groups of people who could use your gifts in their lives. Look for nonprofits or church groups that help them.
- **Volunteer behind the scenes.** Offer to clean the office, do admin work, update the site, or otherwise do the thing no one wants to so that you can have the time to become a student of their needs.

WE WILL BUILD BRIDGES, NOT WALLS

- **Ask yourself, "Who is my 'other'?"** Who, when she or he speaks or shows up in your life, causes cognitive dissonance?

Sit with the Lord and imagine that person deeply loved by God. See the Lord, hold that person, and call them "son" or "daughter." Let that give you patience to wade through the discomfort.

- **Thank God for Jesus.** Remember how you've been reconciled to God through Jesus. Once a day for the next week, pray a prayer of gratefulness for Jesus' inclusive love that brought you in.
- **Resist divisions.** Learn from someone who holds a perspective different from yours. Diversify your bookshelf, podcast feed, and the group of people you follow on social media.
- **Reject systems that exclude.** Consider the groups and events in which you and your family are involved: sports teams, small groups, school events, businesses. If there is a place that openly rejects people for arbitrary reasons or makes participation difficult for some, abstain and call out those groups and events.

WE WILL CHOOSE ORDINARY ACTS OF PEACE

- **Find your small within the big.** Make a list of all the big acts of justice you've always wanted to be a part of. Ask yourself what they all have in common. (For example, I've always gravitated toward organizations that help families and women, so I resolved to devote time to caring for the families and women in my life first before volunteering with a global organization.) Think globally, act locally.
- **Practice "customer service shalom" for one week.** Everywhere you go, notice the names of the people who serve you, make eye contact, call them by their names, and always end your interactions with a sincere thank you. Make it specific: "Thank you, Marge, for giving my daughter a lollipop while we waited in line." This will open your eyes to the people around you for whom you can be a peacemaker.
- **Examine your heart.** When you are interested in volunteering with a nonprofit, consider your motivations. Are you doing it because you genuinely feel a connection to their mission? Or are you doing it because you think it's the "right" thing to do?

If you're not sure about your answer, say no, and pray. Wait until the Holy Spirit illuminates to you that (a) you have an authentic love for the people who are being served, or (b) you feel a sober conviction telling you that it's just pride at work.

- **Remember that every day prepares you for Someday.** Someday there will be a march, a food drive, a campaign, a cross-country move. Someday a larger-scale opportunity will come to practice peace. When it comes, you want to be ready to say yes with an authentic love for people instead of a yes out of fear or a sense that you "should."

WE WILL SHOW UP, SAY SOMETHING, AND BE STILL

- **Prayerfully reflect on Galatians 6:2:** "Carry each other's burdens, and in this way you will fulfill the law of Christ."
- **Identify your solidarity style.** Make a list of all the ways you can carry a Sista's burdens when she is suffering.
- **Consider going on a Sankofa Journey.** I attended my first Sankofa Journey with my denomination, the Evangelical Covenant Church. The denomination's website describes the Sankofa Journey as "an intentional, cross-racial prayer journey that seeks to assist disciples of Christ on their move toward a righteous response to the social ills related to racism. This interactive experience explores historic sites of importance in the Civil Rights movement and sites of oppression and inequality for people of color, while seeking to move participants toward healing the wounds and racial divide caused by hundreds of years of racial injustice in the United States." My compassion and desire to share in the suffering of women in my life grew on that trip.
- **Join a cross-racial conversation in your community.** Some good examples are Be the Bridge (Beabridgebuilder.com) and The Mosaic Project (Mosaicproject.org).

WE WILL BE PEACEMAKERS, NOT PEACEKEEPERS

- Spend some time thinking about the difference between peacekeepers and peacemakers. Which approach is most common in our world? Most natural to you? Do you use anxiety to make decisions? How can you let love guide your decisions instead?

- **Make a list of the vengeful thoughts you've had in the past week.** Dr. Martin Luther King Jr. once said, "Nonviolence means avoiding not only external physical violence but also internal violence of spirit. You not only refuse to shoot a man, but you refuse to hate him." What does an internal violence of spirit look like in your life?
- **Pray for the people or circumstances on that list.** Ask God to bring them peace.
- **Support peacemakers on the global front.** My favorite is the Preemptive Love Coalition, led by Jeremy and Jessica Court-ney. Preemptive Love is a movement of peacemakers who seek the shalom of some of the most war-torn countries by rejecting fear with practical acts of love. You can learn more at PreemptiveLove.org.

Shalom Recipes

Hey, Sistas,

Here are a few of the recipes mentioned in the book. I want you to know that I'm an optimistic cookbook reader. I swoon over glossy pages like I swoon over Mr. Darcy—I know he'll never be mine, but the reading is still fun. Occasionally, though, a recipe works, and when it does, it shows up every week in the Moore house.

These recipes and techniques are tried and true, but they're also incredibly flexible. You can add a dash or a pinch—it's up to you. You can omit or flourish. Whatevers, clever Sista. I chose these recipes because they mirror the life of a peacemaker: we need to find what works for us. Sure, there's a method, but within the method we have freedom. The way of Jesus is narrow, but we're free to be ourselves along it. Wanna skip? Get your skip on. Wanna amble and take your time? Go ahead, girl. Wanna sprint like Peter toward the tomb? Awesome! Do you, Sista. The same is for these recipes. Do you, Sista. Do you. And share on Instagram: #ShalomSistaCooks.

RED BEANS AND RICE

(Chapter 2)

Receive the praise and adulation of anyone who comes for dinner. Revel in how much you have saved on your grocery budget. Remember that you can embody the culture of the kingdom of God right here, right now.

Beans

- 1 pound dry kidney beans
- ¼ cup olive oil
- 1 large onion, chopped
- 1 green bell pepper, chopped
- 2 tablespoons garlic, minced
- 6 cups water
- 2 bay leaves
- 1/2 tablespoon Cajun seasoning (start with that and add more seasoning to your taste)
- ½ teaspoon cayenne pepper (optional)
- 1 pound andouille sausage, sliced (or ham hock, or bacon)

Rice

- 4 cups water
- 2 cups long-grain white rice

1. Rinse beans, then soak overnight in a large pot of water.
2. In a skillet, heat oil over medium heat. Cook onion, pepper, and garlic in oil for 3–4 minutes.
3. Rinse beans and transfer to a large pot with 6 cups water. Stir cooked vegetables into beans. Season with bay leaves, Cajun seasoning, and cayenne pepper (if desired). Bring to a boil, then reduce heat to medium-low. Simmer for 2½ hours.
4. Stir sausage into beans and continue to simmer for 30 minutes.

5. Meanwhile, prepare the rice. In a saucepan, bring 4 cups water and rice to a boil. Reduce heat, cover, and simmer for 20 minutes. Serve beans over steamed white rice.

PLAYDATE TOAST AND SPREADS
(Chapter 12)
Because I'm scared of inflicting anaphylactic shock and burned hands when I host a playdate, I almost always make toast. Here are my favorite recipes for Any Fruit Jam and Lavender Honey. All are amazing on toast made using your favorite bread. With the lavender honey, I like to drizzle it over a piece to toast with a cream cheese spread. This is definitely for the moms, not the kiddos! Make extra honey to add to your lemonade or tea. This also makes a fun gift to give the mom after your awkward post-playdate chat.

Any Fruit Jam
- 3 cups fruit (blackberries, raspberries, or strawberries)
- 3 cups raw cane sugar
- water (varying amounts—see below)
- lemon juice (varying amounts—see below)
- a couple of pats of butter

1. Put the fruit into a preserving pan or large, heavy saucepan. For blackberries, add 3 tablespoons water and 1½ tablespoon lemon juice; for strawberries, add 3 tablespoons lemon juice (no water); for raspberries, add nothing. Bring to a boil.
2. Lower the heat and simmer until fruit is soft and mashable. For blackberries, simmer for 20 minutes; for raspberries, simmer for 4 minutes; for strawberries, simmer for 7 minutes.
3. Slowly add the cane sugar and stir over very low heat until the sugar dissolves completely. Raise the heat to achieve a rolling boil. For blackberries, boil for 10–12 minutes; for raspberries, boil for 7 minutes; for strawberries, boil for 20–25 minutes. Don't stir until the mixture reaches 220°F.

4. Remove from heat, skim off the top layer of fruit, then stir in a couple pats of butter across the surface. Allow to stand for about 15 minutes so the jam can settle. Pour into your favorite plastic container—the jam will last about a week. When cool, let the kids label and seal.

Lavender Honey
- 1 cup local honey
- 12–20 dried lavender leaves and/or buds, to taste

1. Heat honey in a medium saucepan until hot. Stir in lavender. (You can also use fresh lavender or essential oil in place of the dried lavender.) Remove from heat; allow to cool. Refrigerate overnight in a covered glass dish.
2. The next morning, place the honey in a saucepan and heat through once again, stirring occasionally. Strain through a mesh sieve into your chosen storage container. (I love using cute Mason jars with chalkboard labels.) Discard the lavender.

STANDARD LEMONADE
(Chapter 14)
Nothing is as satisfying as lemonade. There. I said it. I know it's incredibly provincial and Southern of me, but I have yet to taste a beverage as versatile or complex as lemonade. It's both tart and sweet. It's me: an imperfect peacemaker in a glass.

This recipe makes 2 gallons, one per pitcher. One idea is to make one pitcher Tart Lemonade and the other Lemonade with a Twist.

- 12 lemons
- 2–3 cups sugar
- 12 cups water

1. Juice the lemons to make 2 cups juice. Kids or guests can firmly roll the lemons for you before you cut in half and juice.
2. In each pitcher, combine 1 cup lemon juice, 1 cup sugar, and 6 cups cold water. Stir. Make one pitcher Tart Lemonade and the other Lemonade with a Twist.

Tart Lemonade
Adjust water and sugar to taste. Chill and serve over ice.

Lemonade with a Twist
Add your choice of:
- strawberries (about 2 cups)
- frozen blueberries (about 2 cups)
- lavender honey (about 1 cup and adding when you add the sugar in the standard recipe)
- limes (about 4 limes)

1. If using limes, roll the limes like the lemons and squeeze the juice into the lemonade.
2. Stir. Serve over ice.

Acknowledgments

Alice Walker says that "thank you" is the best prayer anyone could say. Nearly every day I whisper "Thank you, Lord" for the following people.

Babes: I love being your wife on this adventure in peacemaking. Your deadpan questioning pushed me to write a book that I'm truly proud of. Also, thanks for keeping the kids relatively well fed and alive while I worked.

Valerie Weaver-Zercher: You deserve a billion champagne gummy bears in your mailbox every day.

Amy Gingerich, Melodie Davis, and everyone at Herald Press and MennoMedia: This book would not exist without you. I wish I could send a pot of red beans and rice to y'all.

Sarah Bessey: Let's move mountains together and then binge-watch *Doctor Who*.

Denise, Jessica, Hannah, Kim, Michelle, Leah-Beth, Aimee, Amy T., Amy S., Amy P., Maite, Joelle, Naomi, Tamisha, Debbie, Paola, and Virginia: Thank you for praying, being sounding boards, and making sure I practice good self-care.

Brittany, Margot, Natalie, Jude, and Jessica, my beta readers and theology checkers: You are some of the smartest women I know.

Dawn Rice: You are Miracle Max's chocolate-coated pill. Thank you for bringing me back to the page when I felt "mostly dead" from writing *Shalom Sistas*.

NOTES

CHAPTER 1

page 30   Shalom is a "persistent vision": Walter Brueggemann, *Living toward a Vision: Biblical Reflections on Shalom* (New York: United Church Press, 1984), 15.

page 31   "We understand peace to be the absence of conflict": Rob Bell, *Velvet Elvis: Repainting the Christian Faith* (San Francisco: HarperOne, 2012), 107.

CHAPTER 2

page 37   For more on understandings of Palm Sunday, see Marcus Borg, "Holy Week: Two Different Meanings," Marcus J. Borg Foundation, last modified May 7, 2011, www.marcusjborg.com/2011/05/07/holy-week-two-different-meanings.

page 43   "Jesus didn't say that it was a doctrine": "Embodying the Way: With Dave Tomlinson," The Work of the People video, 8:17, accessed April 19, 2017, www.theworkofthepeople.com/embodying-the-way.

page 46   "In the Kingdom of God, we join with God": Sarah Bessey, *Out of Sorts: Making Peace with an Evolving Faith* (New York: Howard Books, 2015), 126–27.

CHAPTER 3

page 48   "It is this Good which we are commanded to love": William Harmless, *Augustine in His Own Words* (Washington, DC: Catholic University of America Press, 2010), 341.

page 49   "Cities are not people": Neil Gaiman, *The View from the Cheap Seats: A Collection of Introductions, Essays, and Assorted Writings* (New York: William Morrow, 2016), 154.

page 53   "Wholeness does not mean perfection": Parker J. Palmer, *A Hidden Wholeness: The Journey toward an Undivided Life* (San Francisco: Jossey-Bass/Wiley, 2008), 5.

page 55   These twelve fall into four distinct relationships: Lisa Sharon Harper, *The Very Good Gospel: How Everything Wrong Can Be Made Right* (Colorado Springs: WaterBrook, 2016), 36.

page 58   "The answer is this": Shonda Rhimes, *Year of Yes: How to Dance It Out, Stand in the Sun and Be Your Own Person* (New York: Simon and Schuster, 2016), 86.

CHAPTER 4

page 62   "When we reach that point": Peter Enns, *The Sin of Certainty: Why God Desires Our Trust More Than Our "Correct" Beliefs*, reprint ed. (San Francisco: HarperOne, 2017), 79.

page 65   "If you want to know who God is": "Look at Jesus: With N. T. Wright," The Work of the People video, 3:44, accessed April 19, 2017, www.theworkofthe people.com/look-at-jesus.

page 70   In his book *Prototype*: Jonathan Martin, *Prototype: What Happens When You Discover You're More Like Jesus Than You Think?* (Nashville: Tyndale Momentum, 2013), 9.

CHAPTER 6

page 88   In her poem "Difficult Names," poet Warsan Shire: quoted in Amanda Hess, "Warsan Shire, the Woman Who Gave Poetry to Beyoncé's 'Lemonade,'" *New York Times*, April 27, 2016, https:// www.nytimes.com/2016/04/28/arts/music/warsan -shire-who-gave-poetry-to-beyonces-lemonade.html.

page 91   Social psychologist Amy Cuddy: Amy Cuddy, *Presence: Bringing Your Boldest Self to Your Biggest Challenges* (New York: Little Brown, 2015), 89.

page 91   "Each time I write a book": quoted in Sarah Ban Breathnach, *Simple Abundance: A Daybook of Comfort and Joy* (New York: Grand Central Publishing, 2009), 304.

CHAPTER 7

page 113   That word *dominion*: Lisa Sharon Harper, *The Very Good Gospel: How Everything Wrong Can Be Made Right* (Colorado Springs: WaterBrook, 2016), 33.

page 113   "And in the Incarnation": Dietrich Bonhoeffer, *The Cost of Discipleship* (London: SCM Press, 2015), 301.

CHAPTER 8

page 119   "American culture, with its typical": Ester Bloom, "How 'Treat Yourself' Became a Capitalist Command," *Atlantic*, November 19, 2015, https://www.theatlantic .com/business/archive/2015/11/how-treat-yourself -became-a-consumerist-command/416664/.

page 121   "The first commandment is a declaration": Walter Brueggemann, *Sabbath as Resistance: Saying No to the Culture of Now* (Louisville, KY: Westminster John Knox Press, 2015), 5.

CHAPTER 9

page 133   Historian Walter Benjamin wrote that history is: Walter Benjamin, *Illuminations: Essays and Reflections* (New York: Schocken Books, 1969), 257.

page 133   "The Bible invites individuals and communities": "50 States of Joy: A Preaching Series," Yale Center for Faith and Culture, accessed April 30, 2017, http://faith.yale.edu/joy/50-states-joy-preaching-series.

page 136   My favorite description of joy: Willie James Jennings, "Theology of Joy: Willie James Jennings with Miroslav Volf," Yale Center for Faith and Culture, YouTube video, 20:28, September 19, 2014, youtube.com/watch?v=1fKD4Msh3rE.

page 137   For joy, as C. S. Lewis says: C. S. Lewis, *Letters to Malcom: Chiefly on Prayer* (Wilmington, MA: Mariner Books, 2002), 93.

page 138   "We were constantly putting things": P. J. Vogt, "Shipped to Timbuktu," episode 28, *Reply All*, podcast audio, June 18, 2015, https://gimletmedia.com/episode/28-shipped-to-timbuktu/.

page 139   Jesuit priest James Martin: James Martin, *Between Heaven and Mirth: Why Joy, Humor, and Laughter Are at the Heart of the Spiritual Life* (New York: HarperOne, 2012), 25.

CHAPTER 11

page 158   "While we as people of God": Nadia Bolz-Weber, *Accidental Saints: Finding God in All the Wrong People* (New York: Convergent Books, 2016), 47.

page 159   "The cross is the coronation": Brian Zahnd, "The Crucified God," *Brian Zahnd* (blog), March 3, 2014, http://brianzahnd.com/2014/03/crucified-god/.

page 159   "By and large a good rule": Frederick Buechner, *Wishful Thinking: A Theological ABC* (New York: Harper and Row, 1973), 118–19.

CHAPTER 13

page 187   "Small is beautiful again": Courtney E. Martin, "Do It Anyway: The Top 10 Ways That the Next Generation Is Shifting Activism," Huffington Post, September 7, 2010, www.HuffingtonPost.com/courtney-e-martin-/do-it-anyway-the-top-ten-_b_707074.html.

page 192   "Most of us will make a difference": Deidra Riggs, *Every Little Thing: Making a World of Difference Right Where You Are* (Grand Rapids, MI: Baker, 2015), 24.

CHAPTER 14

page 198   "Black people love their children": Ta-Nehisi Coates, *Between the World and Me* (New York: Spiegel and Grau, 2015), 82.

CHAPTER 15

page 211   "We do not need guns": Mother Teresa, *The Joy in Loving: A Guide to Daily Living*, comp. Jaya Chalika and Edward Le Joly (New York: Penguin Compass, 2000), 93.

page 214   "The whole point of the kingdom of God": Marcia Z. Nelson, interview with N. T. Wright, "N. T. Wright: On Jesus and Writing," *Publishers Weekly*, November 23, 2011, http://www.publishersweekly.com/pw/by-topic/industry-news/religion/article/49621-n-t-wright-on-jesus-and-writing.html.

page 217   "The nonviolent rhythms of the cross": Preston M. Sprinkle, *Fight: A Christian Case for Nonviolence* (Colorado Springs: David C Cook, 2013), 257.

EPILOGUE

page 220   "As someone who has been paid": Barbara Brown
            Taylor, *An Altar in the World: A Geography of Faith*
            (New York: HarperOne, 2010) 193, 208.

The Author

Osheta Moore is a writer and podcaster in Los Angeles, as well as wife to an urban pastor, mother of three, and economic justice advocate for women in developing countries. Moore has consistently been a voice for peacemaking, justice, and racial reconciliation. Her work has been featured on numerous websites and blogs, including *Sojourners*, SheLoves Magazine, A Deeper Story, The Art of  Simple, ReKnew, and Rachel Held Evans's blog. Connect with her at Shalominthecity.com.

CPSIA information can be obtained
at www.ICGtesting.com
Printed in the USA
LVOW12*1426261017
553881LV00009B/110/P